J O H N   L I D S T

FACE THE PRESS

NICHOLAS·BREALEY
PUBLISHING
L O N D O N

First published by
Nicholas Brealey Publishing Limited in 1992
156 Cloudesley Road
London N1 0EA

in association with
The Industrial Society
48 Bryanston Square
London W1H 7LN
Telephone: 071 262 2401

ISBN 1 85788 005 6

British Library Cataloguing in Publication Data
A catalogue record for this book is available from
the British Library.

Typeset by Dorchester Typesetting Group Ltd, Dorchester,
Dorset
Printed and bound in Great Britain by The Ipswich Book
Company

CONTENTS

Foreword by Sir John Harvey-Jones MBE   1

Introduction   3

PART I: EFFECTIVE COMMUNICATION

Introduction   7

  1: Effective Listening   9

  2: Accurate Interpretation of Body Language   20

  3: Presenting Your Case   50

PART II: HANDLING THE PRESS

Introduction   67

  4: Press, Radio and Television Interviewing:

     The Case For or Against Doing It   71

  5: Television, Preparation and Briefing   76

  6: What Happens on the Day of The Television Interview   91

  7: Handling the Television Interview   103

  8: Radio: Preparation for the Interview   112

  9: Guidelines for Radio and Television Interviews   121

  10: The Press   129

  11: Training Yourself to Face the Press   146

References   155

Recommended Reading

Publications by the same author:

Beyond the Pay Packet. 1992, McGraw-Hill
How to Recruit and Select Successful Salesmen (2nd edition). 1983,
    Gower
Making Effective Presentations (Audio manual). 1985, Gower
Manual of Sales Negotiation. 1991, Gower
Marketing Planning for the Pharmaceutical Industry. 1987, Gower
Motivating Your Sales Force. 1978, Gower
Negotiating Profitable Sales (handbook for the Video Arts)
    film of the same title). 1979, Video Arts
The Sales Presentation (jointly with Peter Kirkly). 1985, Gower
Training Salesmen on the Job (2nd edition). 1986, Gower

FOREWORD

I AM DELIGHTED to have been invited to write the foreword for this book. For many years I have been deeply concerned at the lack of understanding of the role of business in our daily lives.

Despite the fact that so many of us work in business organisations of one sort or another, the general impression in the United Kingdom is that there is an anti-business bias. If there is, the fault must lie unequivocally with those of us who are involved in business itself. If the calling of which we are proud is viewed by many as being dull, and bureaucratic – or even worse, vaguely reprehensible and dishonest, the blame must lie with us. Only you can speak for business as a whole or for your own firm or factory. You get the reputation which you choose to project, and it is no use thinking that good deeds on their own are enough. The days have long since gone when you can carry on your business quietly relying on the reputation of your products to speak for you and your people. There is now so much media attention in our lives, and modern communications are so instantaneous and all pervasive that there is literally no hiding place. I believe, therefore, that all businessmen have to accept the desirability, as well as the inevitability, of being to speak up for their firm, their people and their field of activity. In many cases you may also find yourselves speaking for your country's part in the activities in which you partake.

Dealing with the press and the media is a subject which does not come naturally to anybody. While I am always doubtful about lists of rules there are certain clear common factors in almost every contact with the press that an individual or company has. I was particularly struck by some of the checklists included in this book. I was pleased to find that they lined up with ideas which I had formulated in order to try and learn from my own experiences over the years. Since it is a part of one's job (particularly as a chief executive) to speak for one's company, a bit of time and effort spent trying to do it properly and effectively can only be a good investment. A pretty good place to start would be reading this book. Perhaps because of, what many may consider to be my excessive appearances in the media, I am continuously learning more about the art form involved. I only wish John Lidstone's book had been available many years ago. It would have saved me a great deal of painful learning through the myriad of boobs I have made over the years. Even more to the point when you present your case badly or ambiguously, you not only let yourself down but also all the people who work for your organisation. You are their representative, in many cases the only person who can speak for them and they deserve the best that you can do. Although in the foreword I have concentrated on the later part of the book I found the first part, which deals primarily with those sadly unappreciated skills of listening and body language, to be equally as important. This part of the book applies to every manager or indeed to everybody who is managed by a manager.

Most of our time in business is spent in communication – either in listening, or in trying to persuade others. I had not realised how much theoretical study has been done in this field and how useful and relevant it is to any form of discussion or meeting. I believe that this whole field is one which will be of the greatest possible assistance to every one of us who works with and through people. The art of management is, after all, the art of achieving predetermined goals by the willingly given collaboration of people. Management is a matter of hearts and minds, not a matter of sums. Hearts and minds follow perceptions – and perceptions are the product of communication. It is therefore small wonder that one of the key skills that is looked for in any business manager is that of communication.

Sir John Harvey-Jones MBE

INTRODUCTION

PROMINENT men and women whose views are sought out by journalists are all too often unprepared and unskilled in dealing with the media personnel and lack the confidence to seek out and exploit opportunities that are available to them. This is at a time when the public is now used to a high standard of presentation by media professionals. These journalists are not only skilled at their job but they have all the paraphernalia and are backed by researchers feeding constant prompts into their concealed earpieces if they have a momentary lapse.

The probability of being interviewed has multiplied; journalists are constantly seeking out those who should have answers to key issues and problems, so that what they say can be conveyed to their viewers, listeners or readers. People who are likely to be invited or confronted by the media need to be equipped with the techniques and skills to handle interviews, to be able to make presentations to the media and to be able to discuss questions and issues raised by journalists. For the media, bad news is always good news so it is essential for those who have to deal with or announce adverse news to be able to do so first and fast rather than be taken by surprise.

Those in responsible positions are expected, as part of their job, to be able to conduct press interviews and to be able to broadcast: but if such media opportunities are to be turned to advantage and not to disaster, you must know how to speak well and present your case and how to deal with questions and comments put to you by journalists, fluently, confidently and persuasively. Above all, what the television viewer and radio listener sees and hears must be believable.

By learning a few straightforward rules, by developing skill and technique, you can become a creditable spokesperson for your organisation. Fluency and competence in handling television, radio and press interviews will be an essential management skill for the 21st century.

THE PURPOSE OF THIS MANUAL

It has been designed to help develop knowledge and skill in three areas:

- how to listen effectively and interpret body language;
- how to prepare and make effective formal presentations;
- how to face and handle the media.

WHO IS IT FOR?

This manual has been compiled to help three groups of people in particular.

- directors and senior managers of public and private companies in the public arena, whose work includes the public presentation of their organisation at annual meetings attended by the press and making announcements or tackling matters that have a national or local impact;
- national and local politicians with policies to present and justify and, when these are implemented, to answer for them and defend them;
- anyone involved in public activities whether in business, consultancy work, public service or education who may want to present a case to the media or may be asked for opinions on matters of national, local or specialist importance.

STRUCTURE OF MANUAL

The manual is in two parts:

Part 1 provides a foundation of knowledge and techniques for

- communicating effectively;
- effective listening;
- accurate interpretation of non-verbal communication and body language;
- planning, preparation and making effective formal presentations.

Part 2 concentrates on how to handle the press so that, as a result, you will be able to

- set clear objectives for media interviews and, at the same time, understand those of the media;
- control media meetings and interviews so that the televised, broadcast or published features do not contain nasty surprises of what you said in an unguarded moment and now wish you had not;
- handle sensitive issues so that the correct facts and impressions are conveyed to the public;
- prepare, structure and conduct all types of media interviews.

Finally, I hope that after studying this manual, you will have a better appreciation of the world of the media. Treat journalists like we all, as customers, wish to be treated. Try to understand their needs and objectives and you will succeed, most of the time, not only getting your point across to them but through to the audiences with whom you want to communicate.

PART I

INTRODUCTION

IMAGINE you have just been appointed Operations Director of an international, publicly-quoted, waste disposal group whose services range from collecting refuse from domestic households and hospitals to the safe storage of nuclear waste from power stations.

Your appointment has been published in the Financial Times and the national press. As waste disposal has become such a political issue, particularly in relation to hospitals and nuclear power stations, your appointment results in an early call from the British Broadcasting Corporation's Television News Science Correspondent, James Wilkinson. 'Would it be possible to send an outside broadcasting car down to your office today to interview you, say at 11.00 am?' asks Wilkinson on the telephone.

'Yes', you reply with alacrity, seizing this early opportunity to put your name and company on the map and also achieve a personal first. You have never been on television before, still less ever been interviewed and you have always fancied yourself as a communicator. So here is a chance to correct some of the false impressions which the general public harbours about commercial waste disposal companies like your own.

But hold on a minute. You have just agreed to be interviewed by a professional, with all the backing of the British Broadcasting Corporation. (BBC), who is very well-informed on the recent House of Commons Select Committee's report on waste disposal. By your own admission, you have never been interviewed on television; you have had no training in how to present your case or how to read the mind or possible intentions of an interviewer from his or her movements. What are you thinking about? Was your mind in neutral when you so hastily agreed to be interviewed on television?

May I suggest you do two things straight away. First, ring up the BBC and rearrange the James Wilkinson interview to a later day and time. Secondly, before you agree to do any interviews with the media, spend a little time studying Part I of this manual to provide you with some practical guidelines so that you face the press better prepared than you are now.

The first problem with all human communications is that no-one thinks that there is a problem. Whether we are talking to one person or to a group, we all too often think that they not only *hear* what we say but also *understand*, *agree* with and will *act* upon what they have heard in exactly the way we think they should.

The second problem is that we are not very good at listening, *really* listening, when someone speaks to us and then understanding correctly what we have heard. This is superbly summed up in the following words displayed on a noticeboard in the Pentagon, Washington:

> I *think you believe you understand what you think* I *said, but* I *am not sure you realise that what you heard is not what* I *meant.*

When we are involved in meetings with either one person or a group of people, our success depends not only on how well we have planned them but on our understanding and mastery of three communications skills:

- effective listening;
- interpretation of body language – 'the art of seeing what other people are thinking';
- effective presentation.

In the next two units, the barriers that create problems in listening, how these can be overcome, and how to interpret the thoughts of others from their body behaviour are examined. In the third unit, we deal with how to improve our skills when we communicate to others.

*Some of the material in Units 1, 2, and 3 has been reproduced by kind permission from *Manual of Sales Negotiatio* (1991), Lidstone, J. London: Gower.

1

Effective

Listening

WHY DON'T WE LISTEN?   10

BARRIERS TO EFFECTIVE LISTENING   10

HOW YOU CAN DEVELOP YOUR LISTENING SKILLS   13

CONCLUSION   17

EFFECTIVE LISTENING CHECKLIST   19

Of all the communication skills, listening is the one in which most of us receive no training, are the least efficient, yet use the most!

Research shows that we spend 80 per cent of our lives communicating and about half of that listening. Studies of the four activities used in communication indicate that and yet, perversely, our educational systems give priority in reverse order. Writing gets the most and listening the least attention.

	Listening	Speaking	Reading	Writing
Learned	1st	2nd	3rd	4th
Used	Most (45%)	Next Most (30%)	Next Least (16%)	Least (9%)
Taught	Least	Next Least	Next Most	Most

WHY DON'T WE LISTEN

There are many reasons why we don't listen when people speak to us. In many societies, particularly western ones, children are taught always to try to do better, to excel and to be assertive. So whilst speaking is a powerful means of asserting our will, our views and our authority, listening is too often thought to be a sign of passivity or of compliance. When we speak we feel in control of events or situations. Yet when we are talking, whilst we may satisfy our own needs, we fail to consider the needs of others. Indeed the more we talk the less we learn!

From my observations all over the world and from other professional analyses, those who are good at listening tend to be good at selling, at negotiation and at communicating effectively. It is this effective communication that you will be striving to achieve in your dealings with the media.

BARRIERS TO EFFECTIVE LISTENING

There are many common obstacles to good listening.

1 **The speed at which we speak in our own language.** We talk at between 120-150 words a minute. But the brain thinks at speeds of up to 500 words a minute. The

consequences of this surplus capacity are that the brain uses it to

- judge;
- evaluate;
- compile responses;
- become distracted and often bored whilst listening to the person speaking.

2 Outside distractions

Fatigue, personal discomfort from seating, over-eating or drinking or lack of both, noise, telephone calls, or too much comfort all make it difficult to concentrate on the messages the person speaking to you is trying to convey. Unwanted messages caused by outside distractions keep intruding and superimposing themselves.

3 Interpretation and distortion

The cultural and educational background of the speaker and, in the mind of the listener, the imprecise language he uses, can often mislead. A vivid example of this occurred within my hearing when the death of Anthony Eden (Lord Avon and prime minister of Great Britain in 1955-56) was announced on a television news bulletin in January 1977. On the same programme a tribute was paid to him by a close political colleague, Christopher Soames, who spoke of Eden as being always '. . . such a gay companion'. I knew exactly what Soames meant yet, in the hotel room listening to those same words, another hotel guest said, 'Amazing. I never knew Eden was homosexual'.

Preconceived ideas from one 's own past experience can distort or colour your reception of an idea, particularly if you associate it with one that failed or created problems for you.

Assumptions about what you hear, leading you to stop listening because you think you have heard it all before, can be very dangerous e.g., at the last round of negotiations, the purchasing director said in a loud voice, 'Pricing is **the** critical issue if you are to enjoy the same volume of our business'. 'This time round', he says in a lowered voice in the middle of other matters,' and in relation to the whole package, price is of course a factor to bear in mind'.

4 Personal barriers

These barriers can block your ability to listen even before the speaker has said a word. For example, prejudices

   against men or women;

   against white or black people;

   against people who are neatly dressed/scruffy;

   men wearing earrings;

   women with strong perfume or wearing nail varnish;

or as Emerson put it,

'What you are sounds so loudly in my ears that I can't hear what you say.'

After the speaker has begun to speak he or she may do or say things in such a manner that you 'switch off'.

This can happen because he or she

   uses jargon;

   uses repetitious phrases;

   has a 'class' accent;

   has irritating mannerisms.

Inefficient listening resulting from any one of these barriers can be very costly to you and your company. It may give rise to the following situations, for instance;

- letters to a journalist who is going to interview you containing errors, first because the shorthand or audio-typist did not listen correctly to what you said and, secondly, because you did not check the letters before signing them;

- appointments or interviews having to be cancelled or re-scheduled to other people's inconvenience because you did not **listen** fully on the telephone when told that the journalist would *not* be available on certain dates and **would** be available on other dates!

HOW YOU CAN DEVELOP YOUR LISTENING SKILLS

There are a number of ways to improve listening skills. First, you should recognise that effective listening is hard work and needs your conscious and concentrated attention to succeed.

This is easier to control when media meetings take place on your premises. The effect of distractions becomes particularly noticeable during radio interviews (see Unit 8). First there are **physical** distractions that can impair effective listening, for example,

AVOID DISTRACTIONS

- another conversation taking place in the same room with you half listening to it and at the same time listening to the persons speaking to you;
- telephones ringing in the next office; traffic, trains passing, a police siren wailing in the distance.

Secondly, there are **visual** distractions which can interfere with your ability to listen, for example,

- a glamorous picture on a Pirelli calendar behind the speaker;
- some arithmetical figure almost visible on a flip-chart;
- a chart amongst the papers in front of the speaker that may relate to what he or she is saying.

Face the speaker squarely

PHYSICALLY ATTEND TO THE SPEAKER

■ Sit where you can see and hear the speaker squarely. If you are meeting seated at a round table and someone from the media sits next to you, it is much more difficult to listen when he or she speaks to you.

Maintain good eye contact

■ The good listener maintains eye contact that is neither fixedly staring at one extreme nor evasively avoiding eye contact at the other. You want to avoid being so different in your eye contact from what we are used to that your listener/speaker draws an unfavourable conclusion, 'She gives me the creeps with that piercing stare all the time, or, 'He's a shifty customer. Never looked at me when I spoke to him'. This type of physical behaviour becomes very obvious during television interviews and is discussed in Unit 6.

■ The psychologist, Michael Argyle, has provided, through his extensive studies, figures for the normal pattern of eye contact:

- we look at each other for an average of about 60 per cent of the time;
- about 75 per cent of the time while we are listening;
- about 40 per cent of the time while we are speaking;
- generally our mutual eye contact when we look into each other's eye is only about 30 per cent when we are speaking or listening to a particular person and then in short bursts which average no more than one to two seconds.

■ Eye contact should convey to the speaker the impression that you do not want to miss a word, that you are all ears, and of course you must convey this by not

- sitting back with your arms folded;
- half closing your eyes when you look at the speaker;
- fiddling with your clothes;
- looking at your watch or your nails;
- doodling on a piece of paper.

■ Look at the speaker so that you convey a picture of someone who is relaxed, still, and at peace with yourself, yet alert.

PSYCOLOGICALLY ATTEND TO THE SPEAKER

Due to the differences to which I have already referred between the speed at which we speak words and can listen to them, you must learn how to use your surplus brain capacity effectively when listening.

What is being said?

■ Listen for the speaker's central theme, not just the facts; try to ascertain the meaning behind the words, even decoding what is not said or left unsaid.

■ Keep an open mind and do not start drawing conclusions until you understand fully all that the speaker **wants** to say.

■ Ignore the speaker's clothes, voice, accent, haircut, sex, poor presentation.

■ Watch out for your emotional filters producing a biased attitude either in favour of what is being said or against.

■ Concentrate and listen to the message. When someone is speaking to you, he or she is usually engaged in one of **four** kinds of verbal communications:

1. INTRODUCTORY, *Getting to know you* communication which has the simple objective of building relationships.

2. CATHARTIC communication when someone wants only a sympathetic ear to listen to pent up feelings which must be expressed.

3. INFORMATIVE communication when ideas, statistics, information are conveyed to you.

4. PERSUASIVE communication when the speaker seeks to reinforce or to change your attitudes, your perception, your behaviour.

■ Use that part of your mind, that is surplus to listening to what the speaker is saying, constructively by thinking ahead; make short notes of what is being said so that you can test your understanding and interpretation. Weigh up the evidence used by the speaker. Ask yourself if this is complete or whether something has been left out? Is this a valid comment?

How is it being said?

■ In the next unit we will find out how to interpret accurately what people are thinking (but often not saying) from their non-verbal behaviour, from their body language. Listen to how the speaker conveys what he or she says and observe the physical movements that accompany the words, for example,

- tone of voice – loud, soft, agreeable, unfriendly, sarcastic;
- facial expressions;
- body posture;
- use of hands.

What is NOT being said?

■ As you listen, ask what is the meaning behind the words used? Try and read the meaning between the lines. The hidden agenda may involve combination of the following:

- justifying a decision or course of action;
- sowing seeds of doubt in your mind;
- trying to promote agreement;
- winning personal acceptance;
- concealing emotions;
- hinting at personal needs to be satisfied;
- promoting a viewpoint;
- imposing a viewpoint;
- trying to flatter you;
- gaining support;
- trying to deliberately provoke;
- gaining commitment;
- clarifying own thoughts;
- airing self-doubts;
- releasing frustrations;
- making light of serious position;
- rationalizing a position;
- instilling.

■ When you are concentrating on understanding what is **not** being said, beware of the dangers of listening in total silence. The decision to adopt a non-intervening listening attitude is not very difficult to sustain, but it can provoke the following reactions by the speaker:

- you are not listening;
- you are not interested in what is being said.

Both reactions can result in the speaker distorting, by exaggeration, different words to obtain a reaction and feedback from you to break your silence.

Because of these undesirable consequences caused by total silence, it is better to listen **interactively**. This involves a form of listening which encourages the speaker to communicate with you, but neither diverts the flow of that communication nor causes the speaker to distort what he is saying. This can be achieved by the following actions on your part:

- eye contact with the speaker;

- body gestures that indicate interest and concentration on what is being said;
- encouraging speaker phrases, e.g. 'That's interesting', 'Tell me more about that';
- paraphrasing – restating for confirmation or amendment the sense of what the speaker has said, e.g. 'So, if I understand this correctly, you are saying . . .', or 'in other words . . .';
- note-taking occasionally, rather than continuously, e.g. 'That is a very important point you have just mentioned. Let me make a note of that straight away.'

CONCLUSION

As our listening habits develop more by chance than through any training, most of us are inefficient listeners. Successful meetings with the press hinge upon accurate mastery by you of all facts. When listening

- attend physically;
- attend psychologically to what is being said, how it is being said and what is not being said.

Ask the right questions to ensure that you hear the **full** story before you start evaluating or drawing any conclusions.

Listening is an active occupation which, like friendship, is in constant need of repair. It deserves your concentration, your intuition, your open-mindedness and curiosity, focusing and listening with all your being.

Some common obstacles to listening

■ Making assumptions, e.g. that the subject is uninteresting and unimportant; that you know what is coming.

■ Mentally criticising the speaker's delivery.

■ Getting over-stimulated when questioning or opposing an idea.

■ Listening only for facts, wanting to skip details.

■ Outlining everything.

■ Pretending to be attentive.

■ Permitting the speaker to be inaudible or incomplete.

■ Avoiding technical messages.

■ Over-reacting to certain words or phrases.

■ Withdrawing attention, daydreaming.

Effective listening checklist	
■ want to listen	Listening is hard work and needs to be done consciously and with the right attitude.
■ look like a good listener	Look alert. Have eye contact with the speaker, lean forward and look interested.
■ listen to understand	Keep an open mind. Do not make judgements until you have understood what you have heard.
■ listen actively	Use eye contact, words, encouraging questions.
■ concentrate	Focus your attention on what is said, how it is said, the words used and the gestures and meanings behind them.
■ look at speaker	Maintain eye contact. Look at the speaker's face, eyes, hands and sitting positions.
■ discipline your emotions	Listen to what is being said. Avoid being biased towards or against the speaker because of sex, appearance, accent, presentation or the words used.
■ avoid physical distractions	Choose, if possible, meeting places where ringing telephones, passing traffic and conversations that can be overheard, will not distract attention.
■ do not antagonise	Try to avoid actions, which will cause the speaker to conceal ideas, emotions or attitudes, such as arguing, threatening questions, note-taking in an officious manner, criticising or appearing not to listen.
■ use speaking/ listening difference	Because you can listen faster than the speaker can talk, concentrate your attention, think back over what has been said, make notes and identify the theme behind the words.

CHECKLIST

2

Accurate Interpretation of Body Language

INTERPRETING BODY LANGUAGE 24

CONCERN FOR TIME 24

RESPONDING TO THE TELEPHONE

EYE CONTACT 26

HAND MOVEMENTS 29

SEATED BODY LANGUAGE BEHAVIOUR 35

STANDING BODY LANGUAGE BEHAVIOUR 40

USING SPECTACLES 42

POSTURES 42

CONCLUSION 49

W E do not listen in a kind of mental vacuum. As we
listen we look at the speaker, and the body movements
that accompany the words spoken convey messages to us.
Accurate intepretation of this non-verbal behaviour is an
important skill to develop to help your meetings with
journalists. Indeed, it has been established from
observation of meeting sequences that, it is only by
considering the words spoken and the complementary body
movements, that the progress of the discussion can be
assessed. Furthermore, since most people are unaware of
the tell-tale messages that their non-verbal behaviour
communicates to the listener they are unlikely to control it.

Research has shown that we tend to give greater weight
to the messages that are conveyed by non-verbal behaviour
than to what is spoken. The following figures indicate the
relative importance we give to the parts of a speaker's
message:

Words	10%
Tone	35%
Non-verbal behaviour	55%

Some researchers put the influence of body language on
what is heard when we listen as high as 70 per cent.

Nevertheless, we need to beware of two dangers, first of
jumping to hasty conclusions or of simplifying the array of
human behaviour and, secondly, of reading messages from
single unrelated gestures. I remember an occasion when I
was sitting in on a management workshop session
conducted by someone who was rather pompously showing
off his claimed expertise in reading body language. Turning
to me he said, 'John, I notice that you have your arms folded
and your legs tightly crossed so you are critically weighing
up what I have been saying. Am I right?' 'No', I replied, 'As a
matter of fact my bladder is full to bursting and I am
wondering how soon you are going to finish this session so
that I can get out to the lavatory.' This indicates clearly how
careful you yourself will have to be when appearing on
television. Your body language will be assimilated by all the
viewers and interpreted alongside your verbal message.

Non-verbal aspects of behaviour form about nine-tenths

of meaningful social behaviour but they are also extremely complex. So, although we rely very heavily on non-verbal behaviour in our normal contact with others, to a large extent we are not aware of doing so. Rather like driving a car, it all seems to happen without our needing to think about it and only becomes the focus of our attention when something intervenes.

There are other factors which make the understanding of body language difficult, such as behaviour which is confusing, contradictory or carries more than one message. Equally, much non-verbal behaviour is ignored because it is thought to be meaningless or unintentional.

Finally, non-verbal behaviour may be disregarded because it is not socially acceptable to draw attention to it or to 'use' it in some way.

Because of its importance in helping us to understand those with whom we deal in the media we can, by our own conscious attention to body language, provide ourselves with a wealth of knowledge about people. During a press interview, the words people use are accompanied by complementary body movements.

Body language often belies the spoken words. Words usually follow our planned thoughts. Body language expresses our unconscious emotions and feelings. Therefore you can ask whether what the speaker is saying to you is mirrored by what he or she is really thinking? What he or she is really thinking is conveyed by non-verbal body language. Words can be chosen and expressed with the greatest care and deliberation but facial expressions, the eyes and deportment are far more difficult to discipline.

To understand body language adopt the following six-step approach:

1 Keep an open mind.

2 Observe your own bodily postures and gestures and your changes of mind, moods or feelings.

3 Ask yourself what are my body language behaviours?
- Am I leaning back or forward?
- Are the palms of my hands open or are my fists clenched?
- Are my legs apart or crossed?
- What am I feeling?

4 Transfer this analysis to others' behaviour so that you develop a reliable dictionary of body language messages.

5 Put the messages you receive from body language together with the words spoken and draw conclusions.

6 At a television or press interview, learn to control your own body language so that you reveal to others only those signals you want to send.

To develop your knowledge and skill to recognise non-verbal communication, use this chart with colleagues to record what they say and how they behave bodily, then check with them how accurately you interpreted their body language.

Speaker	Body language displayed	Feelings behind them	Right? Wrong?

INTERPRETING BODY LANGUAGE

Let us now examine the range of signals or body movements that most people display. These non-verbal signals, often called *leaks*, give the sharp observer information which we may often wish to hide since we believe that, to consciously expose our innermost feelings, makes us vulnerable to exploitation or attack. The more unintentional a signal appears, the more it can be taken to reflect the 'real' person. People 'leak' their real feelings through their legs, feet, hands and fingers and particularly eyes.

Your interpretation will be more reliable if it is based on clusters of behaviour rather than on isolated movements, for example;

- eyes, face, head;
- body movements and posture;
- gestures (e.g. hand to face, chin or back of neck).

CONCERN FOR TIME

HUMAN FEELING
Concern for time

BODY LANGUAGE
Openly looks at watch – unconcerned about impact of action on others.

HUMAN FEELING

Concern for time

BODY LANGUAGE

Pretended yawn – attempt to disguise a look at watch.

Concern for time passing

Secretive glance at neighbour's watch – assumes that it will not be noticed. Shy, sneaky attitude. Is this likely to characterise his or her approach to whole relationship?

HUMAN FEELING

BODY LANGUAGE

Concern for time passing

Fiddles with watch or moves hand over watch face – reveals preoccupation with time or another appointment but reluctance to offend by looking blatantly at watch.

EYE CONTACT

The face is the mirror of the soul and the eyes are the most compelling feature of it. Through them we can convey a variety of feelings from boredom to greed, lust to listlessness, interest to displeasure. Just consider how much we depend on our eyes to add to our understanding of what someone is saying when speaking. Not only do we listen to what is said but we look at the eyes of the person talking to us. The extent to which the eyes are important in conveying non-verbal messages can be experienced by closing your eyes for a conversation with another person. Try it out for as long as five minutes and then list the non-verbal signs and cues you have missed. The list will be surprisingly long and could include many of the following:

Amusement	Caution	Fright
Amazement	Confidence	Frustration
Anger	Curiosity	Gladness
Annoyance	Despair	Hope
Antagonism	Disapproval	Hostility
Approval	Dislike	Humility
Boredom	Friendliness	Hurt

Importance	Pleasure	Respect
Indifference	Prejudice	Rudeness
Inferiority	Pride	Sarcasm
Joy	Prudishness	Shame
Loathing	Puzzlement	Sorrow
Modesty	Regret	Superiority
Nervousness	Resentment	Worry

HUMAN FEELING	BODY LANGUAGE
When listening	People tend to look at the person speaking whilst listening than when talking
When pleased	The pupils enlarge.
When displeased	The pupils contract.
Being evasive	An individual looks at the person he is speaking to for only a quarter to one-third of the time.
When more interested in the person than what is being said	An individual will look more at the person speaking. In normal conservations, people only look at one another for about half to two-thirds of the time. Contrary to popular belief, it is abnormal to look at a person who is speaking the whole time.

HUMAN FEELING	BODY LANGUAGE
Acceptance of what is being said	Positively interested look in eyes or look of pleasure; head is up, mouth may be slightly open and sometimes expressions such as 'yes, yes' are made.

Rejecting what is being said	The mouth will be closed or teeth clamped together, the head down and the eyes less open – squinting or looking angry.

HAND MOVEMENTS

HUMAN FEELING

BODY LANGUAGE

Holding back a comment

One or both hands over the mouth accompanied by a frown or grimace.

Interest – Disinterest

Interest: head up, voice up, palms of hands open as arms in upward direction.

Disinterest: Head down, voice down, arms and palms down.

HUMAN FEELING

Conveying feelings of honesty and sincerity

BODY LANGUAGE

Moves close to the other person

Touches the other person on the arm or back

Hands held against chest or one held against heart but with fingers or palm upward.

HUMAN FEELING

Thinking about the
proposition

BODY LANGUAGE

Strokes chin – when it stops, a decision is likely to be made
or action commences.

For those who smoke and are doing so, the cigarette is put
out and he or she leans forward – the signs of a decision
about to be made.

A deep sigh of relief or a deep breath are signs of someone
who has decided on a course of action.

HUMAN FEELING

BODY LANGUAGE

Making a critical comparison of the proposition

Hand on chin with one or more fingers pointing up the side of the face; if accompanied by leaning back in the chair, this signifies doubt or reservation.

Bored or dejected

One or both hands clasp face.

Anxiety/uptight

Wrings hands or clenches fist.

HUMAN FEELING

BODY LANGUAGE

Attempts at self-control

Coat buttoned up, hands held together in front, in immobile stance; sometimes trying to avoid eye contact or staring into space.

Sitting with hands clenched on knees; in a chair with an arm supports, tightly grips both arm rests; ankles crossed.

Defensive

Hands tightly folded across chest, leaning backwards in chair distancing space from speaker(s), with ankles crossed.

HUMAN FEELING	BODY LANGUAGE
Resentful	Leans forward with arms tightly folded and facial expression to match.

Defensive	Head down on chest.

Awakening interest	Head up and an open look on face, head inclined, indicating to you, 'I am interested'.

HUMAN FEELING

Weighing up what has been said

BODY LANGUAGE

Head up, arms loosely folded, hands open or not clenched – could indicate evaluation.

SEATED BODY LANGUAGE
BEHAVIOUR

HUMAN FEELING

Enthusiastic and open-minded about ideas

BODY LANGUAGE

Sits forward, hands upturned, feet flat on ground, knees apart. When this is coupled with leaning forward, it is a favourable signal.

Not convinced, although attentive

Seated, legs outstretched, ankles crossed or one leg crossed over other.

HUMAN FEELING

BODY LANGUAGE

Change in mental attitude

A pronounced change in physical body movement or a new seating arrangement of arms and legs.

Negative change in attitude

Sudden leaning back in chair, touching the nose, folding arms – a negative shift in attitude.

Fingers to corner of eye; head inclined downward.

Fingers to lobe of one ear.

HUMAN FEELING	BODY LANGUAGE

Negative evaluation of proposal or idea

Rubs or touches nose with knuckles of index finger.

Disbelief – you exaggerate your claims

Runs finger horizontally under nose.

Frustration/exasperation

Rubs back of neck with palm of hand or runs fingers through hair; hissed intake of breath through clenched teeth.

HUMAN FEELING

BODY LANGUAGE

Confident/superiority

Head well back, hands clasped behind head and body leaning back in chair, legs extended or resting on desk or on another chair, ankles crossed. Creates a general air of disinterest.

Bored/dejected

Hand supporting head, eyes half-closed; or doodling on pad with pencil.

Wishing to interrupt

Fleeting gestures of fingers raised to mouth indicates, 'I want to say something'.

HUMAN FEELING

Confidence

BODY LANGUAGE

The listener or speaker forms a pyramid with the fingers of both hands.

Leaning back in chair with feet extended and ankles crossed.

Confident and interested frame of mind

Leans back, feet apart, hands locked loosely together across the stomach.

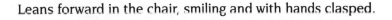

Leans forward in the chair, smiling and with hands clasped.

STANDING BODY
LANGUAGE BEHAVIOUR

HUMAN FEELING	BODY LANGUAGE
Confident – disinterested	Stands hands behind back, shoulders set – 'seen it all before' attitude.

Ownership   Leans against an object such as a wall or door.

Defensive   Buttons up coat, clenches hands, leg on ankle crossed, or an arm crossing chest; dark sunglasses.

Confident approach   Unbuttons coat, takes off glasses, puts down file, unclenches hand, stance open and friendly – secure.

HUMAN FEELING

Assertive attitude

BODY LANGUAGE

Hand shaking – either first to extend hand to you or, by refusing your offer of handshake, puts you at a psychological disadvantage.

First through door when in a group crossing into a room; subordinates fall back for dominant member – often a clue to who holds power in a group.

USING SPECTACLES

HUMAN FEELING

Aggressive resistance to speaker or ideas or both

BODY LANGUAGE

Gains time, usually to answer critically, by sucking end of one arm of spectacle and then folding them and placing in front of the speaker slowly and deliberately.

Slowly and ritually polishs the lens of the glasses – waiting for an opportunity or playing for time to challenge the speaker or stalling before coming to a decision.

POSTURES

HUMAN FEELING

Wanting reassurance

BODY LANGUAGE

Touches tie or signet ring; fiddles with cuff links; twiddles with a bracelet or necklace.

HUMAN FEELING	BODY LANGUAGE

Signs of dominance, superiority or of indifference, sometimes of close friendship

Sits astride a chair with hands resting on the chair back.

Sits in a chair with one leg across the arm or sitting back with both feet on the desk or table in front, ignoring the usual courtesies afforded to a stranger.

Disapproving of what has been said, but reluctant to say so

Sits looking down rather than at speaker, legs crossed picking real or imaginery fluff from clothes.

HUMAN FEELING	BODY LANGUAGE

Reluctant to make a decision because cannot see how problem is to be solved

Head down and with hands and fingers across the eyes.

Eyes closed, head down with fingers pinching the bridge of nose – expect a request for further formation.

Aggressive, defensive attitude

Head down on chest, arms tightly folded, sitting and leaning back with fists clenched and knees together, legs extended and ankles tightly crossed.

Still defensive, but interested

Same posture, but now head is up, legs are drawn up, knees apart, ankles crossed.

HUMAN FEELING

BODY LANGUAGE

Interest developing

Head on one side, fist(s) unclenched, hand on chin, sitting more upright, legs apart and ankles crossed.

Critical evaluation

Similar posture but with finger of the hand pointing upwards along cheekbone, head more inclined, legs apart, ankles crossed.

Openness, enthusiasm, readiness to cooperate

Leans forward in chair, or sits on edge with knees apart and rubbing palms on thigh.

Stands legs astride, hands on hips, coat unbuttoned and swept back, positive attitude saying, 'Let's get going'.

HUMAN FEELING

Readiness to get going

BODY LANGUAGE

Rubs hands together, snaps fingers, hits fist into palm of hand.

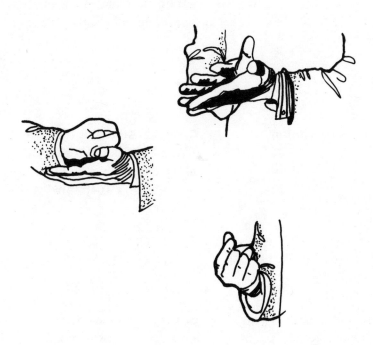

Sits forward in chair, body inclined forward, head up, knees apart, feet flat on ground, forearm across one knee.

HUMAN FEELING

Superior, comparing, authoritative

BODY LANGUAGE

Looks over, rather than through, a normal pair of glasses (not half-moon ones)

Fingers upturned, leans forward on palms of hands for support.

Aggressive, dominant, smug attitude

Hands in coat pockets with thumbs outside and pointing down, coat buttoned up.

Thumbs in waistcoat pockets or hands holding jacket lapels.

HUMAN FEELING

Signals of staged
movement towards a
decision after evaluation

BODY LANGUAGE

Sits upright with one hand on
chin and hand across the
chest.

Followed by head inclined but still evaluating pros and cons
of making a decision.

Signs of staged movement
towards a decision

Sits forward, one hand still on chin the other comes down
with flat of hand on desk. Mentally saying, 'I know what has
to be done'.

The following chart, reproduced from A *Guide to Listening* (Mackay, 1984), provides a useful way of classifying the main types of non-verbal behaviour. Watch out for these in your contact with the media.

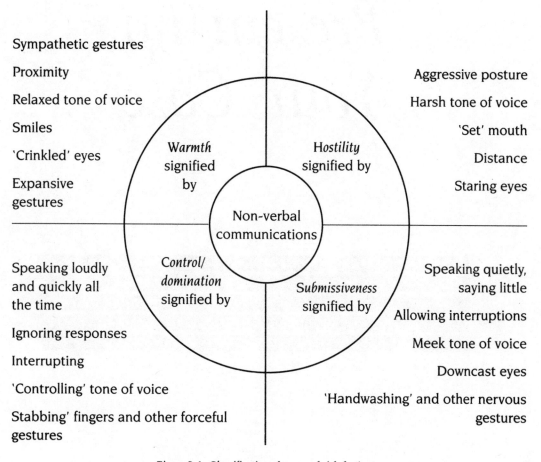

Figure 2.1: *Classification of non-verbal behaviour*

We use our bodies consciously and often unintentionally in communicating by modifying, elaborating and sometimes contradicting the words we use. Correct interpretation of body language is a crucial skill because it enables you to deduce what others are thinking and so smooth the pathway to successful meetings and interviews with the press.

CONCLUSIONS

3

Presenting Your Case

THE MAIN PROBLEMS IN SUCCESSFUL COMMUNICATION 51

HOW CAN WE COMMUNICATE MORE EFFECTIVELY 55

POINTS TO REMEMBER ABOUT EFFECTIVE COMMUNICATION 58

THE LISTENER'S POINT OF VIEW 58

PRESENTATION PLANNING 63

THE MAIN PROBLEMS IN SUCCESSFUL COMMUNICATION

The first problem is to recognise that, despite what many people believe, communicating successfully is not easy.

The second problem is to accept that the onus is on the communicator to achieve successful communication, and not on the receiver.

A number of specific difficulties arise that may prevent the achievement of each of the following communication objectives.

Objective	Difficulties
TO HEAR OR SEE	■ People cannot concentrate for long periods on the spoken or written word. ■ People pay less attention to what appears to them to be unimportant.
TO UNDERSTAND	■ People make assumptions based upon their past experience. ■ Often people do not understand the speaker's jargon. ■ People misunderstand more easily when they hear but do not see. ■ People often draw conclusions before we have finished talking.
TO GAIN AGREEMENT	■ People are often suspicious of others with an interest in selling something. ■ People do not like being proved wrong.
TO INITIATE ACTION	■ People do not easily change their habits. ■ People fear the results of taking wrong action. ■ Many people dislike taking decisions.
TO GAIN FEEDBACK	■ Some people deliberately hide their reactions and what they really think. ■ Appearances can be deceptive – a nod may not always indicate agreement and understanding, it can mask ignorance or indecision.

These difficulties are common to both the communicator and the listener. Neither we who communicate nor our listeners

- like to be proved wrong;
- pay attention to what seems unimportant;
- change our habits easily;
- understand other people's jargon.

THE HUMAN COMMUNICATION PROCESS

If we examine the human communication process we can better understand how it works, how failures in communication arise and what we can do to be more effective and successful as communicators.

The way we communicate is illustrated in figure 3.1. Messages are received through our five senses sound, sight, feel, smell and taste. We then form impressions and assimilate or associate them with other information and ideas stored in the brain. Before we respond to what has been communicated, the brain reacts in a specific sequence to this new information. It scans existing memories of past experiences and finds the frame of reference or memory which relates most closely to the new information received. The new information is sent to join the existing memory bank or frame of reference chosen. If it is associated with what that memory perceived, the new information is analysed and subsequently fitted into the existing memory pattern. As a result of this filing system of the brain, the existing memory may remain the same but stronger, change for the better or change for the worse.

COMMUNICATOR   RECEIVER

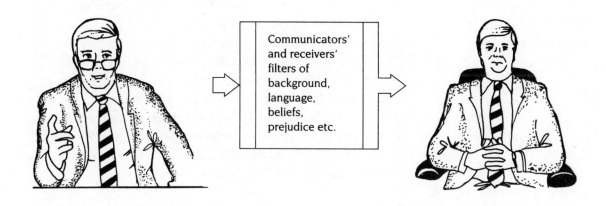

Communicates messages by speaking,
showing, feeling, smell, taste

Receives messages by sound, sight,
feel, smell, taste

Figure 3.1: *How the human communication system operates*

There are constant examples of the results of this
memory bank at work. The politician, whose party is seeking
office after five years in opposition, paints word pictures of
carefully chose unpleasant factors of life which her listeners
will not only recognise but on which (she hopes) they will
agree with her. The chief executive talking to his assembled
management identifies with them as he describes some of
the things he got up to as a young manager.

As well as reinforcing what we believe, other factors can
influence the quality of our communications. There are five
main factors which, as we have seen from figure 3.1, can
lead to failures in communication:

1 the values and standards of communicator and listener;
2 the message being transmitted;
3 the filters through which the message passes;

4 the methods of communication used;
5 the environment in which communication takes place.

THE VALUES AND STANDARDS OF COMMUNICATOR AND LISTENER

Our backgrounds, education, beliefs, ethical standards and prejudices all affect the way we communicate with one another. Thus two people in an audience looking at the same object or picture or listening to the same story may perceive and react to it in quite different ways. Owing to this, it is vital for a speaker to try to perceive the things he wants to say or to show through the eyes and minds of the people who will comprise his audience. The speaker's knowledge of the ideas and experience of his audience will enable him to communicate successfully. Remember this when preparing for media interviews.

THE MESSAGE BEING TRANSMITTED

The same words mean different things to different people. When I was young the word *gay* meant cheerful, full of mirth, exuberantly merry. Today, sadly, it is rarely used in that context but rather as a label for homosexuals, as I indicated on page 54.

Many speakers who have addressed American audiences have discovered that there are enormous differences in the meanings given to words by the Americans and the British. For example, to Americans there is no such word as *fortnight*; they say *two weeks*. We speak about *holidays*; Americans talk about a *vacation*.

Add to these complexities the jargon that frequently creeps into the language of business and the result is confusion. As a general rule in speaking, avoid the use of specialised words – or jargon – because there is a high probability that they will be misunderstood by your listeners.

THE FILTERS THROUGH WHICH THE MESSAGE PASSES

Each person tends to think more often about him- or herself than about the person or group he or she is communicating with or speaking to. The person's words, how they are expressed and the meaning imparted to them reflects this. Yet the individual's own words, prejudices, beliefs and jargon can set up filters which confuse the message sent and received. One simple example of this is the word *media*,

used by an ever-growing number of journalists to mean –
what? To some people it is a word that defines the television
industry; to other people it means radio and to yet others it
signifies the press. Of course, to some people, the word
media is meaningless.

No two individuals hear, see and feel with equal efficiency.
You can tell some people something and they understand
immediately. Others have to be told, shown and then asked
to play back their understanding of what they have heard
and seen before a message gets through. For this reason,
when communicating ideas, a speaker making a
presentation should always involve at least two of the
senses through which listeners receive a message. A speaker
should not only express ideas verbally; some of them at
least – including the important ones for the audience to
remember – become more firmly fixed in the minds of those
in the audience if written down as a handout or shown as a
chart, overhead transparency or slide. For television
audiences consider using a ballooned message below the
picture; for radio listeners, a message may be repeated
twice.

**THE METHODS OF
COMMUNICATION**

The environment can have a profound effect upon the
outcome of communication. If you are addressing members
of an organisation at which different levels of management
are present, what you say is probably going to be digested
at least twice by the junior managers. First, they will hear
what you have said; then they will try to guess how it will be
received by their senior management.

**THE ENVIRONMENT IN
WHICH COMMUNICATION
TAKES PLACE**

When a very large audience has congregated to hear you
speak, it is likely to become almost one person. Indeed
some speakers frame their presentation from the view of
one person. This technique can be an effective one so long
as your research into what your audience comprises and
expects is thorough and accurate.

HOW CAN WE COMMUNICATE MORE EFFECTIVELY?

The communicator's role is that of a teacher educating his

listener to his point of view. This process of helping people to learn can be made much easier by understanding and using the laws of learning: **effect**, **forward association**, **belonging** and **repetition**.

EFFECT

A listener will more readily and willingly learn if your message shows how to satisfy an established need. The 'fireside chats' of President Roosevelt are an example of how to do this. When campaigning for election, Roosevelt used to speak with tremendous effect on the radio to his unseen listeners. He never started by saying such things as, 'I am standing on a programme of this, this and this, so vote for me'. No; he would begin by identifying the basic needs of average Americans and what they wanted: 'You good people of America, you need jobs to provide money to feed and keep your family clothed and to uphold your self-respect, you want. . . .' I have been told by older generations Americans, who listened to these fireside chats, that listeners not only started nodding as Roosevelt spelt out their needs, but then started saying, 'Yes, yes, that's just what I want'.

FORWARD ASSOCIATION

People tend to remember things in the order in which they first learned them, especially if they are arranged in a logical sequence, for example:

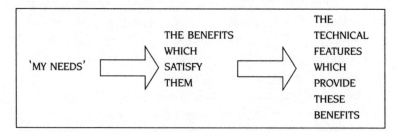

BELONGING

The reason why so many speakers fail to tune into their listeners from the start is the fact that, unlike President Roosevelt, they talk about *their* needs, not the listeners', or they speak about technical features which are quite uninteresting from the listeners' point of view.

People learn more speedily and easily what relates to their own experiences, e.g. 'An air conditioner is like a

refrigerator element with a fan to circulate the cooled air',
or 'The plans I am about to describe are like those you make
for your annual holidays'.

Contrary to what is often thought, constant repetition of a
fact, a statement or a warning does not result in people
learning, as pronouncements about dangerous driving,
excessive drinking of alcohol, smoking etc. testify.
Repetition is only useful as a means of getting people to
learn if it is used in conjunction with one or more of the
three laws already described. A speaker using repetition
plus forward association might say, 'So I repeat what I said
at the beginning of this talk. If you are all really serious in
your wish to cut down road accidents here, then this is what
we have to do . . .'.

REPETITION

Research shows how quickly people forget what they learn:
>   38 per cent in 2 days;
>   65 per cent in 8 days;
>   75 per cent in 30 days.

But they tend to remember things which are important or of
special interest to them. We can help them remember more
by:

REMEMBERING

- ensuring that our first and last impressions
  upon them are both favourable and positive;
- starting a meeting, if possible, by summarising
  progress made at earlier meetings;
- giving them a general idea of a proposition
  before moving on to points of detail;
- involving them from the start by
  talking about 'your problems' and 'your
  requirements' rather than 'what I want';
  obtaining feedback, so that we know how well
  we are communicating, and thus can judge
  whether it is necessary to rephrase our remarks
  or repeat what has been said earlier;
  using more than one sense (e.g. speech plus
  visual aids);
  planning to communicate.

<table>
<tr>
<td>C H E C K L I S T</td>
<td>

Points to remember about effective communication

■ Unless someone *hears* what you say, there is no communication.

■ You do not communicate just words. The whole person that you are comes with them.

■ Talk to people in terms of their own experience and they will listen to you.

■ When you have difficulties in getting through to people, it is a sign that your own thinking is confused, not theirs.

■ When you fail to communicate, it is not your sentences that need straightening out; it is the thoughts behind them.

■ Know what your listeners expect to hear and see before you start talking.

■ Your communication is always more powerful if it appeals to the *values* and the *aspirations* of your listeners.

■ If what you plan to say goes against the beliefs, the aspirations, the motivations of your audience, what you say is likely to be resisted or not received at all.

■ It is not what is written in your notes that matters; it is what percentage comes off those pages and enters the listener's mind and stays there that is important.

</td>
</tr>
</table>

THE LISTENER'S POINT OF VIEW

One of the results of the growth in communications, particularly those involving the visual senses, is that people have become accustomed to certain standards of performance from those who address them. They may not agree with what is being said, they may not even be interested, but they cannot fail to notice the style displayed by the speaker. They remember the image long after they have forgotten the content.

The effect is that it is impossible to say nowadays that any form of presentation will do. For right or wrong, an audience, whatever its composition, will judge an individual's ability and that of his or her company by the kind of job he or she does on his feet. This is not to say that the substance of the speaker's proposals is unimportant, rather that the impact is disproportionately enhanced or diminished by the quality of his or her presentation. You are, in a sense, only as good as the ideas for which you gain acceptance. There are four categories of speakers:

1 Those who do not bother about what they are going to say or how they are going to say it.
2 Those who 'put on a show', but convey very little.
3 Those whose material is good, but badly presented.
4 Those who have something worthwhile to say and present it well.

The judge of a presentation is the audience. No two audiences are the same. The individuals within an audience differ in their attitude, but whatever their personalities and job responsibilities may be, they all react to presentations. There are certain mental demands which have to be met before they will give their willing acceptance. In addition, they are affected by what they see, what they hear and how they feel. All these can be summarised as the listener's viewpoint, whose basic elements form a sequence from which a speaker can prepare a structure for his presentation or interview.

The thinking sequence that listeners' minds follow consists of seven points. A presentation must take note of them all.

THINKING SEQUENCE

1 **I am important and want to be respected** Each member of the audience wants the respect of the speaker. Without it the speaker is lost.
2 **Consider my needs**. Any proposal is judged by the listeners in terms of their own priorities and sense of values. These are determined by what they each want to achieve in their work and as a person.
  The content of a presentation will have little impact if

listeners cannot see that its theme is about improving their lot. In a business context their needs will be concerned with such things as improved profitability, higher sales, lower costs, better industrial relations, etc. They want to know early in a presentation that the theme is of this type. If so, they will give the speaker their willing attention and interest. Likewise, their final decision will rest on the answer to one question: 'Will my needs be met by these people and their proposals?'

3   **Will your ideas help me?** If the listeners' attention and interest have been gained, they are keen to know how the speaker's proposals will help them achieve the end results both themselves and their company are looking for.

4   **What are the facts?** This step in the thinking process arises from the previous one. Listeners want to know how the speaker proposes to ensure that the promised results are forthcoming. Depending on the situation, they may also want evidence that the promised results have been achieved in other cases of a similar nature. They also want to know what their own involvement will be in terms of action to be taken, time commitment, etc.

5   **What are the snags?** It is an integral part of the listeners' decision-making process that they should consider possible disadvantages arising from the speaker's proposals. If any come to mind, which they cannot see being overcome, they will frequently voice them in the form of objections. In a group situation, there is a bigger chance that objections to the speaker's proposals remain unvoiced.

6   **What shall I do?** Provided all previous points have been covered each listener is now faced with the decision to accept or reject these proposals. In making the choice, they will concentrate on their own needs (job or personal) and decide accordingly. If there are several sets of proposals to consider, listeners will prefer the ones which, in their eyes, best meet their own needs.

7   **I approve**. If Points 1 to 6 have been satisfactorily handled from the audience's point of view, they will make a decision in the speaker's favour.

The seven points mentioned above represent the path that the human mind takes before it will give willing approval to proposals. The problem facing speakers, however, is that by nature they have difficulty in presenting their proposals in that kind of sequence and with that kind of emphasis. In many situations where proposals are being presented the speaker is concentrating on his or her own company and ideas while the audience is more interested in what they want to achieve. Consequently, the audience loses interests, their attention wanders, and they reject both the proposals and the speaker.

By structuring the presentation around the listener's point of view the speaker can go a long way to gaining the audience's attention and interest, persuading them of the value to them of his proposals, meeting their objections, and drawing them to a conclusion in his or her favour.

When presented with proposals, the human mind not only thinks along certain lines, it is affected by what it sees and hears. To a lesser extent it is affected by sensations of touch, taste and smell. In formal presentations **sight** and **hearing** are of the most concern to a listener.

Sight. Listeners react to their first visual impact of you as a speaker. They expect your dress, facial expressions, and gestures to match their mood and the content of your presentation. They look for signs of confidence. Consider the position from the listeners' viewpoint.
They see:

- How you are dressed. Are you dressed up in bizarre clothes which will distract your audience from what you say to them? Try and dress neatly and like the group you will be with;
- Your mannerisms. Always be yourself, but avoid distracting mannerisms. Some speakers wave their arms up and down whilst talking, like an air traffic controller. Gestures should be controlled, few and powerful, and used to emphasise specific points.

Listeners find it much easier to concentrate on and take

greater interest in the things they can see. But what they look at must be understandable, simple and professionally handled. They have greater confidence in a speaker who looks at them. Keep in touch with your audience by looking at them.

Hearing. There are two major differences between a public presentation and a normal conversation. During a conversation you can ask your listeners if they understand what you have just said, or alternatively they can ask you to repeat something if they did not hear you or understand. But in a public presentation this is not always possible or there may not be any interruptions. So you have to make sure that you get your message across and understood *the first time*. For these reasons, remember the following points:

■ Speak louder than you would in normal conversation. Adapt the scale of your presentation to the size of the room or hall and to the size of your audience so that everyone *hears* you. However, this does **not** apply when presenting or speaking in a television or broadcasting studio (see Unit 6).

■ Always make sure you pronounce words distinctly and emphasise the last words in each sentence. Inexperienced presenters have a habit of fading at the end of each sentence. If it contains the most important part of your message and no-one hears you, your presentation has failed (see figure 6.1, p. 79).

■ Audiences expect you to speak in language they can understand. Avoid jargon which might confuse people.

■ Do not speak too fast.

■ Vary the pace and vary the pitch of your voice to maintain people's attention and interest.

■ Use pauses. Nothing is more effective in a presentation than the pause. It gives the audience time to digest what you have just said or shown and gives you time to pick up the substance of your next point. It holds an audience expectant of what you will say next.

■ People dislike having to concentrate on a presentation that is merely read out.

Success in all formal communication is founded upon understanding the listeners, looking at what is *said* and *shown* from their point of view and endeavouring to meet their needs. Good ideas, however sound they may be, will not stand alone. They have to be presented **attractively**, **clearly** and **persuasively**. This means combining a listener-based structure with presentational skills so that your whole presentation achieves its objective.

CONCLUSION

PRESENTATION PLANNING

Presentations are selling situations. They are also unnatural social relationships because the speaker

WHY PREPARE?

- has usually sought out the listeners;
- wants them to act in his or her favour;
- may have to replace their ideas with his or her own;
- feels out on his or her own.

These problems create tension, which makes the speaker act out of character by talking too rapidly, avoiding eye contact with the audience and concentrating on his or her own ideas rather than on the audience's needs. Planning helps to reduce tension and ensures an audience-orientated presentation based on *your requirements* rather than *our proposals*.

Since planning is simply the thinking process that precedes purposeful action, the first thing is to choose **your objective**. This can be a long-term objective covering a series of presentations or a single objective for one session. Having got your objective, you can then move to a structure for the presentation proper. For simplicity, this structure should be based on the listener's point of view and divided into three main parts, the **beginning**, the **middle**, and the **end**.

WHAT SHOULD YOU PREPARE?

Listener's point of view   **Preparation points**

I am important and want to be respected. Consider my needs.	Beginning	Getting attention. Building rapport. Statement of theme: audience needs.
Will your ideas help me? What are the facts? What are the snags?	Middle	Points to be made. How they will benefit the audience? Support material: examples; third party references; visual aids. Possible audience objections: answers.
What shall I do? I approve.	End	Résumé of theme. Audience needs. Summary of points Closing words: commitment.

Apart from reducing tension and ensuring an audience-orientated presentation, a structure has other important advantages for a speaker:

- It enables the audience to follow easily, because it is based on an initial outline of the theme, followed by development of that theme. There is a summary of the theme, and the points made, with a request for action.
- It ensures that every mental demand by the audience is covered.
- It provides a framework to fall back on if the audience leads the speaker astray.
- It provides a disciplined and logical basis on which the speaker can plan the presentation.

Sit down at your desk with pencil and notepad and imagine you are already in front of your audience. Ask yourself several questions:

- Who are the audience?
- What are their needs?
- How much do they already know about the subject?
- What do they need to know that I can tell them?
- What are their backgrounds, culture, level of ability?

One of the most important skills to develop is setting down what you want to say in notes, to which you can refer easily. Do not become the prisoner of a sheaf of closely written material with your eyes glued to it as this will not hold the attention of your audience.

For a complicated talk or interview write out what you plan to say in detail. Then select the key sentences or words that summarise each section and put these either on to cards or into checklist form on paper. Then take your notes and not your lengthy first draft with you; the notes will be easy to refer to without making you their prisoner.

PART II
Handling the Press

INTRODUCTION

In the following units, I describe how you should analyse, prepare yourself for and handle press, radio and television interviews.

Before you study these units, first complete, as far as you can, a personal questionnaire of your perceptions of the media. The questionnaire has been designed so that you can record not only your perceptions, but also notes of any firsthand experiences you have had of being interviewed by the media and the problems you encountered or perceived.

At the end of this manual, you will be asked to fill in a photocopy of the original questionnaire. Try to complete this one as well, but only **after** you have read the preceding units. The reason for asking you to do this is so that you can compare the two questionnaires to see if your perceptions have changed as a result of a better knowledge and understanding of what journalists do and how you should face up to and handle the media.

PERSONAL MEDIA PERCEPTION QUESTIONNAIRE

My Personal Perceptions of the Media

Ratings: For each medium tick the rating that most closely represents your personal perception.

PRESS

	VERY	SOMEWHAT	INDIFFERENT	SOMEWHAT	VERY	
1 is sympathetic to my organisation/industry						is antagonistic to my organisation/industry
2 is objective						is biased and gives one-sided coverage
3 gives fair treatment						is manipulative
4 is well-prepared						is superficial
5 shows understanding of my organisation/ industry						lacks understanding of my organisation/ industry

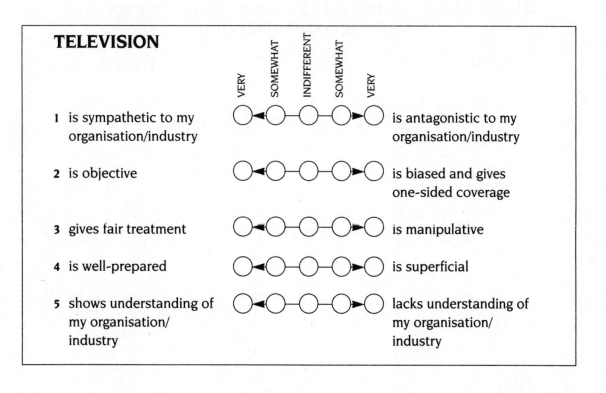

MY PERSONAL PERCEPTIONS OF THE MEDIA

PRESS	RADIO	TELEVISION

MY PERSONAL EXPERIENCE AND PROBLEMS FACED IN HANDLING THE MEDIA

PRESS	RADIO	TELEVISION

4

Press, Radio and Television Interviewing:

The Case For or Against Doing It

FACTORS FOR DOING THE INTERVIEW 72
FACTORS AGAINST DOING THE INTERVIEW 73
COOPERATION WITH THE MEDIA 73

THE decision whether or not to appear on television or take part in a radio programme is like any other management decision and should be made in the same way. When you are asked to give a press, radio or television interview, always weigh up the pros and cons of doing so.

C H E C K L I S T	Factors for doing the interview
	• a public relations opportunity: • enhances the organisation's status in the community; • provides free promotion for the organisation; • promotes a positive organisational identity for personnel recruitment. • interviewing practice • opportunity to inform or influence public opinion • opportunity to correct or prevent misunderstandings • staff motivation • opportunity for self-projection to increase likelihood of being asked again • opportunity to put your organisation's case versus that of the competition • opportunity to change public attitudes • opportunity to influence specific target group(s), such as financial institutions, scientists, etc.

	Factors against doing the interview
C **H** **E** **C** **K** **L** **I** **S** **T**	• an unpleasant experience • time pressures • lack of time to prepare • you are not the right person to do it • danger of putting up a poor show • you do not want to disclose your organisation's policies or plans at present • you do not want to be exposed to being brow-beaten or made to look foolish • company culture • pressure from your colleagues • danger of your views being distorted • loss of the comfort of anonymity • possible danger of threat to your career • bad for stock market timing

COOPERATION WITH THE MEDIA

There is everything to gain and nothing to lose by cooperating with the media and building up a fund of future goodwill with journalists.

Often, when journalists get in touch with you, they are going on a fishing expedition, searching for information or the names of reliable people who could take part in a programme or provide specialist advice. All journalists have a little black book of best sources of information. Becoming a journalist's source of good information or be able to recommend good people they can contact is a valuable exercise. When journalists have tested your recommendations and found them reliable, your advice will be sought again. In recommending other people to do a particular programme if you are not the best person, do not worry that you may be passing up an opportunity. Better to miss the opportunity this time round than to be the wrong person and risk looking foolish. An occasion may arise where, when asked who is the best person to do such and such an interview, you can say, 'Well, you are talking to him – I am'.

Never underestimate the positive value that can result from taking part in a programme. An example of this occurred when I was directing a training programme for a group of senior sales representatives employed all over the world by Imperial Chemical Industries (ICI) at their residential training centre, Warren House, Kingston-on-Thames. It so happened that Terry Wogan had persuaded the then chairman of ICI, Sir John Harvey-Jones to be interviewed by him on one of the evenings of that week. No senior member of this company had ever appeared on such a television programme before, let alone the chairman. Sir John was very fluent, very amusing and, as he has often demonstrated since, a superb ambassador for his cause and company. The effect on that group of ICI staff was electric. In the space of about ten minutes, Sir John did more for the morale of the staff than all the pep talks that top management could have given.

If you decide against cooperating with the media or decide not to appear, then you would be well-advised to give the journalist, radio or television company a carefully prepared statement on your point of view. Then, if reference is made to your non-appearance, you have at least provided material that can be quoted. Additionally, if it is not used or is misquoted, you have a proper basis for complaint, using such methods as letters to the press or television programmes like *Right to Reply* and similar radio versions. You always have to balance the decision not to cooperate against the danger of providing the media, or your competitors, with a free run at your expense. Sadly, however good your reasons, when a commentator makes the comment, 'We invited a spokesman from . . . to appear on this programme, but they declined', viewers and listeners are likely to conclude, 'So what are they trying to hide?'.

If you decide to cooperate with the media, or in circumstances when there is no option but to do so, then your preparation must be thorough: **prepare, prepare** and again, **prepare**. Never play it by ear.

Also remember the great difference between written and spoken words. What may read quite well, may not come off the page and sound so good when spoken.

Having balanced the advantages and disadvantages, or if you have no option but to agree to be interviewed or to appear as your organisation's spokesperson, then what should you prepare? This question is dealt with in the next unit.

5

Television: Preparing and Briefing

DECIDING TO DO THE INTERVIEW 77

GATHERING INFORMATION FROM THE MEDIA 80

YOUR PERSONAL PREPARATION 81

PREPARATION FOR HANDLING CRISIS SITUATIONS 84

W HEN you are approached by any of the media to comment or to contribute to a programme, you have to decide whether to do it or not. Even if special circumstances leave you with no option, **do not give an immediate answer**. Say that you will call back within 30 minutes and make sure that you do as journalists have a high regard for people who can be relied on to meet deadlines and always do. Use the time that you have bought to seek advice within your organisation as to whether to do the programme and, if the answer is yes, then who ideally should do it.

	Deciding to do the interview
C H E C K L I S T	ASK YOURSELF AND COLLEAGUES: ■ Will the organisation benefit from taking part in the programme? ■ If so, are you the best or most appropriate person to do it? ■ Are you available to do it? ■ Do you have the necessary knowledge and skill to do it? ■ Does your company want you to do it?

ASK THE MEDIA

■ What do they want to get out of the programme?

■ Why do they want me to do it?

■ What role would I be expected to play?

■ Will the programme take the form of an interview or will I be a member of a panel or discussion group?

■ Who will be the interviewer?

■ What do I know about the interviewer or panel?

■ When will it take place?

■ Where will it take place?

■ What is the name and status of the caller?

■ What is the name and telephone number of the producer and director of the programme?

■ How long will the programme last?

■ Who decided to do this programme and why?

C
H
E
C
K
L
I
S
T

CHECKLIST

WEIGH UP:

■ The plus and minus points.

■ You are under no obligation to give an interview.

■ Unless there are compelling reasons against it, be inclined to say yes.

■ If your answer is going to be 'no', you should have a good reason that can be quoted to the media if need be.

Gathering information from the media

RETURN THE JOURNALIST'S CALL AND FIND OUT:

■ Why are the media doing this article, broadcast, programme?

■ Why have they contacted me?

■ What questions will they ask? Do not be surprised if you do not get a definite reply to this question. They are not simply being evasive. Often they prefer only to outline what the programme will cover in case giving you a list of precise questions might lead you into giving parrot-like replies that will rob the programme of spontaneity and flow.

■ Is there a hidden agenda for the programme? You might not get a straight answer to this question, but you can draw your own conclusions from vague or evasive replies.

■ In what context will my contribution be used?

■ Will the programme be 'live' or recorded?

■ If recorded, will it be on film or videotape? (Film is used for magazine programmes rather than for news items.)

■ Will film or props be used or required? They are an added complication, so beware. Great preparation and rehearsal is needed.

■ Who else will be on the programme?

■ Why will others be there? Could I be used as the 'fall-guy', as a scapegoat for what has gone wrong?

■ What questions will they ask?

■ How do these questions relate to the stated objective(s) of the programme?

CHECKLIST

In unit 3 entitled *Presenting Your Case*, there are useful tips on preparing yourself. Here I want to emphasise the following points that you should bear in mind:

<table>
<tr><td rowspan="2">**C H E C K L I S T**</td><td>### Your Personal Preparation</td></tr>
<tr><td>

■ For a five minute interview set aside at least one hour for preparation. The importance of preparation is emphasised on page 49.

■ Plan to say what you want to say, not what the media want you to say.

■ People usually remember up to three points, so do not put over more than three. If there is one point that is more important than any other, keep this one to the last. Then, if the viewers or listeners only remember one, they are likely to remember this one. Most people are not effective listeners.

■ Likewise, never make more than three sub-points.

■ Use brief, memorable anecdotes. Relate a fact to a memorable story to aid the listener (see page 44).

■ Use analogies, for example, the length of a cricket pitch rather than 22 yards; the height of London's Telecom Tower rather than 580 feet. Visual pictures are easier for the audience to relate to and consequently remember.

■ Learn your brief and stick to it. Then you will always have something relevant to say and to fall back on as a framework. Look back to the discussion on structure on page 50.

■ Never use jargon. The specialist words and language used between people in the same field of operations at work may not be understood by anyone else. Similarly, avoid using abbreviations, initials or acronyms that could well be meaningless to other people. The example on page 3 illustrates the pitfalls of jargon and colloquial speech.

</td></tr>
</table>

ANTICIPATE THE INTERVIEWER'S ANGLE.
LIKELY QUESTIONS CAN BE DEDUCED FROM:

**C
H
E
C
K
L
I
S
T**

■ What they said would be asked.

■ Put yourself in the shoes of the interviewer. What questions would you ask yourself about the subject?
NB: Few journalists have any business knowledge or experience. Their background is usually the media and their career objectives are different from yours. Never assume that they are motivated by the same factors as you are.

■ The interviewer does **not** have the right to ask you questions outside the subject matter. If this happens, do not answer them. Ensure that the journalist returns to the subject and the questions relevant to the programme and to your brief.

■ Do not be defensive or apologetic. Use the journalist's questions to get your own message over. Use their questions to your advantage. Mrs. Thatcher was skilled in responding to a question by saying, 'I'm glad you asked that question. It underlines the point I want to make which is . . .' Remember not to present defensive body behaviour either (see page 23).

**C
H
E
C
K
L
I
S
T**

DRESS AND APPEARANCE:

■ Avoid wearing new or trendy clothes. Wear non-contrasting clothes that will not distract the viewer's attention. It is difficult to ignore these types of distractors (page 6) which are obstacles to effective communication.

■ Be your presentable self.

■ Avoid narrow stripes or bold checks in clothing that might prove distracting or very broad stripes.

■ Do not wear flashing jewellery that might catch the strong lighting for a television interview. For a radio programme, do not wear anything that might jangle and be picked up by the microphone.

■ Wear light, pastel colours as they are better than dark colours on television.

■ If you wear spectacles, keep them either on or off: There is nothing so distracting as someone who is always removing them whilst speaking. Also this type of body language conveys conflicting messages (see p. 32). Never, never wear dark glasses.

PREPARATION FOR HANDLING CRISIS SITUATIONS

When you are interviewed, it is often a problem to say what you want in the limited time available. This is especially the case on television. There is no time for long-winded explanations. You can only make statements.

Yet such statements need to be the result of meticulous preparation. Nowhere is this more important than in crisis situations.

The following checklists have been reproduced by permission of Peter Tidman. They originally appeared in the MCB University Press Selling and Management Series, Volume 5, No. 2, 1988. Creating a checklist is a useful way of preparing yourself to *face the press* in a crisis situation.

The checklist presented in figure 5.1 was produced for an oil company which was subjected to a major catastrophe exercise by the Department of Energy in 1986. Some 67 issues were raised to which oil company executives had to resolve their statements. When the Department of Energy inspectors carried out the exercise, they raised less than half the points listed for which statements had been prepared but a checklist like this allows you to be adequately prepared to face the interview.

Similar models have proved of immense value to organisations involved in crises such as a take-over bid, the privatisation of a car manufacturer, the Airtours disaster at Manchester Airport, public enquiries on Stansted Airport or Sunday openings of retail stores and the withdrawal of a major pharmaceutical product following research.

There may also be cases where the misfortune of one operator in an industry may spill over and affect every other manufacturer. It is vital then to put the record straight about the safety of your own operations. And of course the importance of giving good interviews to the media is paramount. Unfair though it may be, in the mind of the public, you can be guilty by association. The media will pose the question of how your own organisation would tackle the situation or problem. Anticipation of the issues which may arise and preparation of your answers (see figures 5.1 and 5.2) will help you to pre-empt any nasty surprises coming from the interviewer or any other protagonists in the studio.

Figure 5.1: **Issues raised in an in-company exercise – catastrophe at an oil platform**

Fire at night – shut down and get off the platform

1. What happened?
2. Is it contained?
3. Any casualties?
4. Head count (200).
5. Who is missing?
6. Evacuation by helicopter/boat.
7. Helicopter time to hospital/ashore.
8. Boat time to hospital/ashore.
9. Burns unit.
10. Emergency services ashore.
11. Spokesman at emergency centre.
12. Radio/telex/tied lines to incident room.
13. Tied line/telex to Press Centre from incident room.
14. State of seas.
15. All lifeboats launched (radio in lifeboats).
16. Any visitors out there?
17. Can helicopters land on platform?
18. Pollution threat.
19. When will fire be contained?
20. What are you doing to find missing people?
21. What about NOK*?
22. Who is informing them (police)?
23. Will there be an explosion?
24. Danger to other platforms out there.
25. How long can men survive in water in survival suits?
26. Extra helicopters searching (Bristow).
27. RAF helicopters available.
28. NIMROD availability?
29. Help from other oil companies (Sector Club).
30. What went wrong?
31. Who is to blame?
32. Past incident record (Ensure you annotate all previous incidents)
33. Other major incidents elsewhere.
34. Medical facilities on 'Stand-by Boat'.
35. Is there a doctor on 'Stand-by Boat'?
36. Any nurses on 'Stand-by Boat'?
37. Any help from Frigg field (30 miles)?
38. Any other ships/trawlers in vicinity to help?
39. Any Royal Navy ships in vicinity?
40. Is this sabotage?
41. Any evidence available?
42. Previous threats.
43. What happens to NOK* if men lost?
44. Can wives (NOK) see their men?
45. Do you have welfare people to visit NOK*?

*Next Of Kin

46. Do you have transport to help NOK see their men?	56. Effect on UK supplies?
47. Compensation for personal losses.	57. Who will put out the fire?
	58. Fire control.
48. Health and safety checks.	59. Cigarettes, pipes, cigars.
49. When last done?	60. Sleeping quarters.
50. What did they say?	61. Cookhouses.
51. Was everything implemented?	62. Chip-pan fires.
52. Are the men fit for tasks/emergencies?	63. Any drugs around?
	64. Type of chemical extinguishers.
53. Who is now in charge?	65. Security checks.
54. Where is helicopter?	66. Terrorist or sabotage threat.
55. Production restart.	67. Structural integrity of platform.

Reproduced with kind permission of Peter Tidman from *Broadcast Communications*, (1988). Northampton: MCB University Press.

The checklist below shows the interview model prepared by the management of a water company in anticipation of the privatisation of the UK water industry. The quantity and quality of the water available was questionable in the light of the drought of 1976 and the contamination of supplies in Cornwall and elsewhere. Apart from these issues, the decision to privatise water was controversial and unpopular politically. The company therefore decided to prepare itself for every eventuality the media could throw at it. The media, as expected, was on top of the situation.

An outsider was used to help executives brainstorm the types of questions the media might be expected to ask. The resulting checklist of interview questions is reproduced in figure 5.2 by permission of Peter Tidman, 1992:

Figure 5.2: **UK water privatisation – a case study**

- What changes will occur on privatisation?
- You will have the same people, technologies and procedures so how will you improve your operations?
- How will you inject a new motivation into people?
- Are you looking for high flyers to join you?

- Your government dowry is £150 million and your debts are £400 million. How will you clear those obligations?
- Will you manage your finances better in future?
- Will the same financial managers be in charge?
- Why should you do better this time around?
- Will there be financial training?
- Why are you still discharging aluminium sulphate into your rivers, despite the experience in Cornwall?
- How do you deal with runoff of agrochemicals and pesticides?
- How do you deal with industrial pollution of the water supply?
- What happens to runoff from sludge spread on the fields?
- Why do you allow 40,000 tonnes of sludge a year to be dumped off-shore?
- Why have you banned canoeists on your rivers in favour of Yuppie anglers?
- How are you handling discharge from fish hatcheries?
- What are you doing about discoloration of the water supply?
- How are you combating scum, bubbles and worms in water?
- Is fluoride safe?
- Why are you spending £30 million a year on television commercials?
- Are you cooperating with *Friends of the Earth*, the *Pure Water Society* and other groups?
- Is radiation in the water a threat to health?
- Why is the cost of water likely to soar?
- What about the 25 per cent of your customers who already find charges too high?
- Are you contracting out labour?
- What are your managers doing to relate to the local communities?
- What is the policy on water meters?
- How much will they cost?
- How long will they last?
- Why aren't you making meters yourself?
- What reserves do you have for product liability emergencies?
- Can anthrax infect the water supply?
- Why do we run out of water during the shortest dry spells?
- What have you got show for all the money spent since the big drought of 1976?

- If you've spent thousands of millions making reservoirs safer, does that mean they weren't safe before?
- How can you justify pushing up charges just to pay dividends to shareholders?
- What about redundancies to reduce the wage bill and push up profit?
- Why are sewers suddenly collapsing all the time?
- Are there dangerous reptiles alive in the sewers?
- Can they come up through the lavatories?
- What are you doing about the growing rat population in the sewers?
- Does our water supply carry Weil's disease from rat urine?
- Is there a danger of sewer explosions from methane?
- What about hydrogen sulphide?
- What is happening to industrial water rates?
- Are you going to charge for clean water going in and effluent going out?
- Why do you give discounts to well-off people who pay in advance?
- Is water contaminated with heavy metals from industry?
- What are you doing about lead pipes in old houses?
- Do washing machines have check valves to prevent soiled water getting into the water supply?
- Are we getting lead poisoning in areas where the water is acidic?
- Are manganese levels too high?
- What will happen to all the land you own when you are privatised?
- Are you going to build desalination plants?
- What will they cost?
- Who will pay for them?
- Are you going to diversify?
- Can AIDS from hospitals infect the water supply?
- What are you doing to prevent Legionnaires' disease?
- Is there Hepatitis B in the water?
- What about botulism?
- Is your water causing a kidney stone epidemic?
- Why is there such a high cost of Escherichia coli bacteria in the shellfish in your area?
- What about silage discharges from farms?
- Are you planning any more dams or reservoirs?

- Are your groundwater sources polluted?
- Do you have enough staff to monitor abstractions?
- Are you going to sell what was public land to developers?
- Are you going to restrict land access to ramblers?
- What is going to happen to your salary costs when you go private?
- Is the government turning a blind eye to water problems by agreeing to accept lower standards from privatised companies?
- What will Brussels say to violation of European standards?
- How are you making managers more commercially aware?

The managers of the water company did not stop at the creation of this list and rehearsing answers to the creation of this list and rehearsing answers to the questions they had identified. They also came up with a useful list of words and phrases that were to be avoided in any media contact, either because they are jargon, technical shorthand or merely executive mumbo-jumbo. In their particular business, the list included the following:

- *potable water*
- *other units*
- *raw water*
- *indicators*
- *new water bodies*
- *fixed charge basis*
- *abstraction*
- *acidification*
- *alleviation schemes*
- *bathing use areas*
- *conjunctive use*
- *design criteria*
- *determinations*
- *discharges*
- *dispositions*
- *EC designated beaches*
- *desalination*
- *deepols*
- *Dwrpols (pollution of the Welsh river Dee)*
- *rotacuts*
- *singular points*
- *license*
- *scrutinise and approve*
- *single points*
- *statutory objectives*
- *freedom to discharge*
- *low flows*
- *organic*
- *pathogens*
- *point sources*
- *precepts*
- *riparian owner*
- *specifiers*

- *overtopping*
- *mode of transmission of water*
- *fixed parameters*
- *plethora*
- *tankering*
- *boilers*

6

What Happens on the Day of The Television Interview

GETTING TO THE TELEVISION STUDIO 92

WHAT TO EXPECT AT THE TELEVISION STUDIO 92

WHO DOES WHAT AT THE TELEVISION STUDIO 93

YOUR NOTES 98

VOICE TEST 98

NERVES 99

VERBAL BEHAVIOUR IN FRONT OF THE CAMERA 100

PHYSICAL BEHAVIOUR IN FRONT OF THE CAMERA 100

TIPS: WARNINGS AND ADVICE 101

IF it is your first experience of appearing on television, you are likely to feel both excited and nervous. Do not be tempted to go to a party the night before to take your mind off the morrow! You will need all your wits about you.

GETTING TO THE TELEVISION STUDIO

Ensure that you allow yourself extra time for the journey so that you do not arrive at the studios in an agitated state. It is often much more sensible to ask the studio to look after all your travel arrangements in both directions. This will not involve you in any expense as it is in the interests of the programme organisers to get you there. They cannot afford for you to be late.

WHAT TO EXPECT IN THE TELEVISION STUDIO

MAKEUP

For television only, expect a certain amount of makeup. This is likely to be no more than a light powdering to reduce face shine and the red in your complexion. However, even this may not happen, as studios aim to portray more and more natural situations on television.

MEETING THE INTERVIEWER

If you are told that you cannot meet the interviewer until the actual interview, clarify the reasons why not. If you are not satisfied with the explanations, do not appear.

If you are a man and the interviewer is a woman, or vice versa, there should be no difference in how the interview is conducted.

Go over the ground to be covered in the interview or whole programme.

INTRODUCTIONS

Make sure that the interviewer has a written note of your name, correct business or other title and your position in the organisation beforehand.

If your name is open to more than one pronunciation, tell the interviewer exactly how you wish to be introduced. I once had to interview a man whose name on paper was spelt 'onions', like the root vegetable. When I met him and welcomed him as 'Mr Onions', he immediately corrected me and said that his name was pronounced, 'O–ny–ons'.

As I have already indicated in the checklist on page 70, it is less common now for a producer of a programme to want to do a complete dummy run by going over all the questions that will be put to you. This is not because they want to confront you with any knock-out questions, but rather to avoid spoiling the spontaneity of the discussion.

DEFINE THE LINE OF QUESTIONING

WHO DOES WHAT AT THE TELEVISION STUDIO

At the television studio there will be a variety of people engaged in making a programme; the editor, the producer, the director, the floor manager, the camera crew, researchers and secretaries. The explanatory notes below, together with the studio diagram in figure 6.2, p.97, should give you a better understanding of what all these people do. **Let all these people do the worrying, not you**.

STUDIO PERSONNEL

❶ **The production assistant** provides organisational support to the director during the preparation of the programme and during studio operations, assisting with the timing of the programme (which is termed 'calling the shots') and subsequent editing and dubbing.

❷ **The vision control engineer** is responsible for the electronic set-up of the cameras, working closely with the lighting director to ensure the best conditions for camera performance.

❸ **The lighting console operator** is in charge of an electronic lighting memory system which is preprogrammed to operate the appropriate lamps at the right time during recording.

❹ **The scene hand** assembles and positions scenery on the studio floor, moving the different sets when needed.

⑤ The camera operator operates the camera itself on the director's instructions, following a prearranged camera script which gives the order of camera shots.

⑥ The sound boom operator positions the microphone suspended on the end of the boom to make the sound compatible with the picture, i.e. quiet for distant shots, louder for close-ups.

⑦ The lighting director decides the positions, strength and any special colours of the lighting to provide the best conditions for the cameras and to enhance the creative aspects of the set and artists. The lighting director also supplies special lighting effects if required.

⑧ The lighting electrician places the lamps in position on their telescopic arms, adjusting them when necessary.

⑨ The floor manager makes sure that everything and everyone is in the right place at the right time on the studio floor, co-ordinating all activities and relaying the director's instructions to artists. The floor manager maintains contact with the control suite by short-wave radio talkback. Remember that the floor manager is in charge so put yourself in these capable hands which are being paid to look after you. Let him or her do all the worrying instead of you. Ask to be taken through the whole procedure, for example, where to sit and who does what. If you want anything, just ask for it.

⑩ The stage manager ensures that everything on the set is in its designated place both before and during recording, attending to the finer details.

⑪ The floor assistant aids the floor manager, ensuring that those participating in the programme are on the set when needed and giving them cues when it is their turn to appear or to speak.

⑫ The producer has overall responsibility for the

programme, deciding the content, sometimes choosing the leading artists, and handling organisation, administration and finance.

⑬ The vision mixer operates the vision control panel which cuts and fades pictures and gives special electronic effects, controlling pictures displayed on a bank of monitor screens. There is one for each camera being used, one for prerecorded or filmed inserts and another for captions or still photographs.

⑭ The operations supervisor is responsible for the technical and operational quality of both sound and vision, ensuring that all remote facilities such as video recorders or telecine machines are on hand. This may entail liaising with Master Control if a programme is going out live.

⑮ The sound supervisor balances one sound against another, ensuring that the quality of sound matches the picture by adjusting the tone and volume controls, and directs sound operations in the studio.

⑯ The grams operator plays in sound effects and music on cue, which are mixed with the speaker's dialogue from the studio floor. Many effects are added during later *dubbing* operations.

⑰ The director who works in the studio or in the control suite, translates the script into action on screen, directing actors and camera operators, then supervising videotape editing and sound dubbing after the actual recording.

⑱ The designer researches the particular period of the programme to create the sets, draws a floor plan, constructs a working model and also decides the content of the set.

⑲ The props hand 'dresses' the set with furniture, pictures or curtains and supplies items such as books, food or telephones if they are required by the designer.

20 **The wardrobe dresser** 'dresses' the actors with costumes designed by costume designers to reflect the period accurately. Costumes are made by the costume department.

21 **The makeup artist** enhances the features of actors with makeup, ageing them or making them look younger, styling hair and applying special effects such as artificial blood, wigs and scars.

Fig 6.2: **Studio layout diagram**

YOUR NOTES

If you feel more secure with notes to hand, then just take a pad or cards with a few **large printed stab headings** on it. Never take whole sentences written down in long hand as when you glance down they will be difficult to read. You are warned against becoming a prisoner to your notes on page 50.

Make sure that the clipboard or pad on which your notes are written can be held or balanced easily on your knees or on a chair arm.

Try to avoid the necessity to read from your notes all the time. It will lose you the interview with the viewers because you lose eye contact and with it your credibility.

On questions of fact, a statistic or an important quotation, then refer openly and quite confidently to your notes, reading out the specific figures or passage in measured words.

VOICE TEST

Nothing is more upsetting than being all keyed up to answer the first question put to you by the interviewer only to find that you have lost your voice or, worse still, have a frog in your throat making you splutter out something incoherent. Having sat in on film sets many times as a technical director, I have a tip for you. Before filming takes place many directors ask the actors on the set to have a really good cough to clear their throats. It works, so do not hesitate to do the same, having checked beforehand that the red light for recording is not on.

You will be asked to take part in a short technical rehearsal so that the technicians can do voice and camera tests. Do not say much and, above all, do not use this occasion to rehearse your opening words or an answer to a question.

VOICE PITCH

For the routine voice test, speak as normal. Do not shout, but be sure to keep the pitch firm and clear at the end of each sentence. Beware of the *English fade*. This is the tendency to tail off at the end of a sentence. See figure 6.1.

Be sure to pronounce the last words in each sentence clearly and at full pitch because they often convey the most important part of what you want to say.

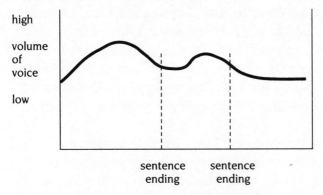

Figure 6.1: **English fade.**

NERVES

Speaking in public and doing it well is a social skill. Since we all want to give a good account of ourselves, we care very much how successfully we carry out this social skill. As a result, most people feel nervous at the start of an interview in which they are going to participate and also at the end. How can you minimise these two problems?

BE WELL-PREPARED

■ By preparing answers to the types of opening questions that are likely to be put to you and then rehearsing by speaking through how you will deliver those answers.

■ By preparing an opening statement that is short and clear and rehearsing it so that you are word perfect and do not have to refer to any notes to prompt you. If you do this you will be looking at the interviewer and thus at the viewers and the result will be a picture of confidence.

■ By preparing a short final statement which you have rehearsed so that, if and when the interviewer turns to you and says, 'In 30 seconds could you sum up your case', you can respond to this invitation clearly and confidently.

PACE OF TALKING

 SPEAK SLOWLY

Speak at a slightly slower pace than in normal conversation. In conversation, we speak at about 130–150 words a minute, so slow down to about 100 words a minute. Slow right down to about 60–90 words a minute when talking to an audience of mixed nationalities whose first language is not English. Remember that, for most of them, they need to translate what you say back into their own language before full understanding is achieved.

STYLE

Speak in short sentences. The shorter the sentence the better. If the programme in which you are participating is recorded, it is much more difficult to edit short sentences. Broadcasting is different from public speaking. It is not speech-making any more than it is personal conversation. There is no time for explanations, otherwise you will court the cut-off, 'Sorry, but we must stop there', leaving you dangling in mid-air with an unfinished and probably incomprehensible jumble words as the viewers' final impression of you.

 BE PRECISE

Television time is expensive. So get straight into the subject as a newspaper headline does. On average a television interview in a news programme lasts about two and a half minutes, with your input to it probably not lasting more than about 60 seconds. On radio, a spot on the BBC news programme *Today* averages about 15–30 seconds. So there is no time for such preliminaries as, 'First I would like to thank you for the opportunity to speak to all your listeners', — you are speaking to them, so get on with it!

Keep to **spoken** English rather than that used for writing.

POSITIONING

If you have a 'good side' that makes you look better than the other, then let this be what the viewers and the interviewer see.

Sit forward in your chair. In this position you will feel alert and, what is equally important, you will look alert when the camera starts to roll. Your posture conveys a great deal

about your attitude as the illustrations in unit 2
demonstrate.

Avoid swivelling or comfortable chairs into which you can
slump down.

Sit still with your shoulders square to the interviewer.

Do not look at the camera, look at the interviewer. Talk to
the interviewer and you will be talking to the viewer or
listener because it is the studio technicians' job to ensure
that this happens.

Avoid flitting eye movements which, however unfairly, are
regarded as a sign of being sly and shifty. Wherever you look
or whomever you look at, do so for long enough to appear
as though you mean it. Conversely, don't have a fixed glazed
look like a rabbit outstaring an oncoming 15-ton truck.

EYE CONTACT

LOOK AT THE ☑
INTERVIEWER

MAINTAIN NORMAL EYE ☑
CONTACT SEE p.5

If you want to emphasise a point with your hands, do so
provided it is not excessive like the windmill gyrations of the
television broadcaster, Doctor Magnus Pyke. Your hands are
a part of your personality so let them work for you.

GESTURES

TIPS: WARNINGS AND ADVICE

Do not drink any alcohol before the programme even if it is
offered to you in the hospitality suite of the studios. Even
the slightest slurring of your voice will become very obvious
on television.

ALCOHOL

NO ALCOHOL

Be on your guard from the moment you enter the studio
until you leave it.
When talking to the interviewer before the programme goes
on air, watch out that you do not say things like:

'This is not in my notes, but . . .'
'Although I am not going to say this in the interview. I feel . . .'
'This is off the record, but . . .'
'You won't be asking about . . . will you?'

BE ON YOUR GUARD AT

Nothing is off the record to the ambitious interviewer who
wants to make a name for him or herself.

**NOTHING IS OFF THE
RECORD**

Those of you in the United Kingdom or elsewhere where the popular BBC programme, *Yes Prime Minister*, has been shown on television, will perhaps have seen the one in which Sir Humphrey is interviewed by Ludovic Kennedy. At the end of a dreadfully dull and stilted interview, Sir Humphrey sighs with relief, then thinking that the recording is over, says what he really thinks. Out comes some juicy and scandalous Civil Service gossip. The only snag is that he failed to notice that the red light was still on, recording his every word taped for a future broadcast.

Always remember that at the studio you are on enemy territory. Everyone there is a potential news gatherer, aware that nervous people often speak unguardedly.

Be on your guard if you are put into a reception room or hospitality suite and left there on your own for some time. Such isolation, coupled with nervousness, can loosen the tongue and result in you giving unintentional ammunition to the interviewer.

BE NAIVE

If you have been inside a television or radio studio before, beware of passing yourself off as a 'professional' who knows all the ropes. You may then be left to your own devices and come a cropper.

Let the floor manager and studio staff show you to your seat and fix the microphone clips to your clothing. They have done this hundreds of times so let them get on with it.

MAKE REQUESTS

If you are unhappy about any aspect of the studio such as the chair you are sitting in, the way some lights are shining on your face, or you feel that you may want a glass of water available during the interview, then say so.

☑ BODY LANGUAGE
INDICATES SINCERITY:
SEE p.20

SINCERITY

Never tell lies on television. It is a cruel medium that will unmask the liar and hypocrite in ten seconds flat.
Be yourself. However, if you have a very quiet personality, then you may have to inject some additional enthusiasm to project yourself to the viewer.

7

Handling the Television Interview

EXPLOITING SILENCE 104

ANSWERING QUESTIONS 104

DEVELOP A POSITIVE APPROACH 105

VERBAL STYLE 106

MANNERISMS 107

TIPS: WARNINGS AND ADVICE 107

SELF-ASSESSMENT 108

DIFFERENT TYPES OF TELEVISION INTERVIEW 109

GUIDELINES TO REMEMBER WHEN BEING INTERVIEWED DOWN-THE-LINE 111

EXPLOITING SILENCE

During a television interview, it is the interviewer's responsibility to keep the interview going, not yours. If a silence ensues after one of your answers, then it is his problem to deal with the situation.

After you have finished answering a question, some interviewers will deliberately remain silent for longer than is necessary, to provide a trap for unwary interviewees to implicate themselves.

If you have no clear objective for the interview or a specific mental picture, you will be tempted to fill the vacuum of silence created by the interviewer by saying things you did not plan to say.

ANSWERING QUESTIONS

  LISTEN: SEE PAGE 3

PAUSE

 DO NOT EMBROIDER ANSWERS

Listen carefully to the whole of the interviewer's question without interrupting.

Pause to give yourself time to compose your answer, then answer the question.

Do not be afraid of pausing before answering if a totally unexpected or difficult question is put to you. Remember pauses always seem longer to you than to your audience. However, there is a difference when speaking on radio and this point will be covered in the next unit.

Hesitate or pause only if it is deliberate.

Do not overembroider your answers to questions. Know your own limits of knowledge and expertise and do not talk about anything of which you know little or nothing.

Always know your facts or have them to hand in your notes.

One of the easiest ways to compromise yourself is when the interviewer allows you to go on talking.

 SHUT UP

When asked a question, answer it. Say as much as you need to say, then shut up. It is the interviewer's problem to cope with the silence that could ensue, **not yours**.

Remember that the art and skill of interviewing is to only speak for about ten per cent of the time and to let the interviewee speak for the other 90 per cent.

If the interviewer rephrases your statements or answers, make sure it is accurate. If not, correct the misapprehension immediately and do not let the interviewer move on until you are satisfied.

CORRECT MISUNDERSTANDINGS ✓

When answering questions put to you by interviewers, do not let them interrupt or butt in. **Stand your ground**. Alternatively, give way to the interviewer and then, when they have finished interrupting or harassing you, continue with your previous answer as though they had not spoken.

HANDLING INTERRUPTIONS ✓

Do not lose your temper or get involved in a verbal brawl. For the programme director's monitors it makes great television, but not from your point of view as it is at your expense.

KEEP CALM ✓

Refute any incorrect statements made by the interviewer or anyone else taking part in the interview immediately and firmly. Do not even consider answering the next question until you have done so.

REFUTE ERRORS ✓

At the start of an interview you can, if you prefer to and feel more comfortable, mention the name of the interviewer. But do not address him or her continually by name.

Remember that it is to the viewer or listener that you are talking.

DEVELOP A POSITIVE APPROACH

Do not apologise.

DON'T APOLOGISE

Television interviews are seldom as bad as you imagine when heard or seen from the listener's point of view. If you have made a mistake or you have to correct a fact, then do just that and move on without apology. This applies to live interviews.

When an interview is being filmed or taped for a later broadcast and you make a mistake, do not hesitate to stop, explain why you have done so, and insist that your error should **not** be included in the transmission. The director then has two options, either to do the piece again or abandon the whole interview.

STOP AND ASK TO RETAKE ✓

Do not get sidetracked by the interviewer.
Do not volunteer irrelevant information.

KEEP TO THE SUBJECT ✓

LOOK ALERT AND
INTERESTED: SEE PAGE 34

Look alert even when you are not the subject of a question (as happens in a panel discussion).

 BE PREPARED FOR
SURPRISES

Try to prepare yourself for any surprises, e.g. a film clip, some statistics thrown at your or the sudden and unforewarned introduction of another studio guest.

 DON'T LET YOURSELF BE
PUT ON THE SPOT

When this happens, avoid being put on the spot or answering the questions arising from this twist in the programme. Let the viewers or listeners know that these surprises have been sprung on you, but show that you can handle them.

VERBAL STYLE

 NO JARGON: SEE PAGES 11
AND 54

Do not use jargon, abbreviations or colloquial English. As mentioned in Part I of this manual, jargon comes from anyone who works in a specialised field of activity. As a result you get into the habit of speaking jargon to those who work with you and therefore readily understand your shorthand. To the layperson outside that confined, specialist circle, your language is gibberish.

You often see this happen when armed services personnel, civil servants and politicians speak. Abbreviations are used such as UNESCO (United Nations Educational, Scientific and Cultural Organisation), NEDO (National Economic Development Office) and LDCs (Less Developed Countries).

YOUR AIM IS TO
COMMUNICATE
EFFECTIVELY SEE PAGE 51.

Slipshod words and phrases like *cool*, *no way* and *at this point in time* can all be meaningless to many people. If they do not understand what you are saying then, as a communicator, you have failed.

Put yourself in the shoes of the average listener or viewer and imagine how they think, feel and speak. Make what you say understandable to them and you will be communicating to everyone.

MANNERISMS

We all develop mannerisms of one sort or another. And until we appear on a television programme or take part in a radio broadcast, we are never made aware of them unless we have frank friends or plain-speaking families.

Avoid prefacing the beginnings of your answers to questions with too many fillers like, 'wells', 'aha', 'umm' and 'yes'. Unless what you say is compelling, your unseen audience will start counting the fillers instead of listening to what you are saying.

AVOID FILLERS

Do not tail off your answers with expressions such as, '. . . and so on', '. . . and so forth', '. . . etc., etc.'. They are irritating and meaningless.

Do not have continual eyeball to eyeball contact with the interviewer. It is uncomfortable for you both and also looks completely unnatural to the unseen viewers and listeners.

NATURAL EYE CONTACT:
SEE PAGES 16 AND 48

Repetitive mannerisms, either verbal or visual, distract the listener or viewer from what you are saying.

DON'T FIDGET SEE PAGE 4

Visual distractors include lip-licking, wriggling in your chair, folding and unfolding your arms, removing and replacing your spectacles, scratching your ear and running your finger across your nose.

Verbally, the constant use of particular phrases distracts, for example, 'I mean . . .', 'With great respect, but . . .', or 'The fact of the matter is . . .'.

TIPS: WARNINGS AND ADVICE

Assume that you can be seen and/or heard throughout the broadcast and immediately afterwards.

EVERYTHING IS RECORDED

Make sure that the broadcast, or recording is **over** and the recording machinery is switched off.

For the same reason, keep still in your seat and avoid the temptation to lean forward to speak to the interviewer or anyone taking part in the programme.

Remember that the programme director in the control room has television monitors of everything that happens. There will be no hesitation in exploiting and recording an unguarded yawn, a raised eyebrow or a disgusted look to the ceiling which may be used to add colour or help make the television programme more compelling. Your feelings are the least of their worries.

EYE CONTACT

Look at the interviewer or another programme participant when they are speaking to you.

Beware in particular of looking away halfway through a question addressed to you. It will convey the impression that you are not listening, even if you are. If you break your eye contact, look **down** rather than up to left or right and then look back at the interviewer. No-one looks at another person for more than a few seconds at a time.

THE 'LAST WORD'

Do not try to score points.

Always remember that the professional interviewer has control of the last word and is likely to win.

Watch out for the interviewer getting in a harmful last word. Know his final timing deadline for the programme. Armed with this you can sometimes lengthen your last reply to shorten his opportunity for expansive and potentially harmful comments.

NERVES

Nerves, that tingle of apprehension, those butterflies in the stomach, are signs that you care about what you are going to do. The opposite feeling of over-confident, can be lethal.

ADMIT IGNORANCE!

If you are asked a question about a particular matter and you do not know the answer, do not be afraid to admit your ignorance.

SELF-ASSESSMENT

Listen or watch the programme in which you have participated as objectively and critically as you can and assess your strengths and weaknesses against the items listed in this unit on handling a television interview.

Check off the points on your planned brief for the programme. How many of them did you get over as you planned? Look back at the *effective communication checklist* on page 45. How do you rate yourself?

1 National news programmes

If you are asked to appear on a national news programme because of your involvement in a matter of current importance or because of your specialist expertise, it is likely to be a brief rather than a lengthy input.

News items average one to two minutes. So every second counts. After the news reader or interviewer has introduced the news item in which you will participate, there will probably only be about five to ten seconds left for your comment or answer to a question. Therefore, every word must count and none must be wasted.

2 Local news programmes

In each television region, after the national news ends, there follows a regional magazine-type programme made up of topical, local news items. Should you have an opportunity to take part in such a programme, you will usually have more time in which to air your views. In addition, the interviewers tend to be less aggressive than those you meet on the national news networks.

Nevertheless, be factual, use short sentences and answer questions simply and briefly. A good performance can lead to further interviews — remember the interviewer's 'black book'.

3 Documentary programmes

These take the form of well-researched, in-depth handling of a specific subject. The programme maker will probably devote many days or weeks to background research. If you are asked to take part, it will be because you bring equally specialist expertise to the subject that is being examined.

You need to have a clear, written brief on your contribution so that you know what to prepare and what will be expected of you.

Often, your contribution takes the form of perhaps one hour's interview. If the programme is recorded, your contribution may end up as no more than a total of five minutes, divided up into three or four excerpts of 30–60 seconds which have been extracted from that one hour interview.

4 Current affairs programmes

These take many forms. The best known ones are *Panorama*, *On the Record* and *Weekend World*. If you are asked to take part in any one of them, **be on your guard**. Such programmes rely on dramatic revelations for their impact and appeal.

If the studio making the programme has an axe to grind or a biased viewpoint to peddle, you should ask yourself whether you should even be thinking of taking part. If you do so, go for a live interview where there can be no editing of your contribution. Then prepare yourself, very thoroughly.

5 Specialist subject programmes

These usually deal with only one subject or functional area such as finance. Such programmes include *The Money Programme* or *European Community*.

6 Down-the-line participation

Although this is dealt with in unit 8 relating to radio, television brings with it special factors that you need to be prepared for.

The television studio, in which you are installed, is usually a small one, some distance away from the interviewer. In it there will be a television camera and sometimes an operator, but not always. It is like one of those photograph booths where you can get passport-type photographs taken. If the television camera is unmanned, it will be operated by a remote-controlled joy-stick.

The interviewer is miles away. You, in your booth, are connected to the interviewer by means of a British Telecom line or microdish. You cannot see the interviewer but you can hear his remarks and questions, usually through an earplug or speaker.

This unnatural situation results in the startled and sometime wooden expressions you see on the faces of people being interviewed from these down-the-line studios.

**C
H
E
C
K
L
I
S
T**

Guidelines to remember when being interviewed down-the-line

■ Look directly at the television camera lens.

■ Keep still throughout the interview.

■ Do not look at the television camera lens all the time because it becomes very tiring and difficult.

■ When you look away from the lens, look down at your notes then back to the lens. Never look upwards.

■ Sit upright and sit forward in your seat so that you look alert.

■ Sit square to the camera lens.

■ The camera lens will highlight every aspect of your appearance so, before the television goes live, ensure that

- your hair is neat
- your clothes are ironed with no creases
- if you are wearing dark clothes, any hairs or specks are removed as they will be magnified by the camera.

The camera tends to highlight such things and results in the viewer remembering what you looked like rather than what you said. Consult the checklist on page 71.

8

Radio: Preparation for the Interview

DIFFERENCES BETWEEN RADIO AND TELEVISION INTERVIEWS   113

WHO IS YOUR AUDIENCE?   113

SELF-PREPARATION FOR A RADIO INTERVIEW   114

TYPES OF RADIO INTERVIEW   117

FIVE TIPS FOR RADIO INTERVIEWS   120

Whilst many of the points I have already made about television interviewing apply to radio as well, there are some radio appearances which raise some specific issues which are dealt with in this unit.

DIFFERENCES BETWEEN RADIO AND TELEVISION

On television, viewers not only hear what you say, they can also see you. On radio, listeners can only use one of the senses. They can only **hear** what you say.

On radio, listeners **listen** to the message; the visual picture does not get in the way.

Radio is often a more friendly medium than television; the interviewer is not normally trying to best the interviewee.

Radio is much cheaper than television, so the opportunities for extended interviews in which you can put your full case are greater.

There has been an explosive growth in local radio in the last few years. This has resulted in radio stations frequently employing young people at the start of their broadcasting careers. Consequently they will often be younger than the people they are interviewing and usually ignorant about commerce and industry.

Due to the recent growth, there are more opportunities for you to develop links with your local radio station. Indeed, if you are in a specialist field of activity, there may be an opportunity to become a regular source of comment.

WHO IS YOUR AUDIENCE?

When you are invited to take part in a programme, either for an interview or perhaps to make a brief 15-second comment on the *Today* programme, always ask yourself, 'Who listens to this programme?' Successful inputs are usually made by those who are able to become **personal to the listener**, who come over as though 'they are speaking to **me**'. The importance of considering audience needs is discussed on pages 46 and 50.

AUDIENCE NEEDS: SEE
UNIT 3

For this reason, beware of pigeon-holing or categorising your listeners into groups such as retailers, housewives, children, consumers, the young, the elderly, bankers and motorists unless the programme is a specialist one directed at one of these groups. If you do categorise, then all those who are not in that group or do not perceive themselves to be in the group to which you appear to be speaking, will switch off.

 TALK ABOUT 'YOU'

On radio, always talk about 'you', because for the listener that means 'me'. Never use 'one', 'I' or 'we'. These terms all draw attention to yourself and away from your listener. Remember, a bore speaks about himself; an interesting person is one who speaks about other people.

When you are asked to take part in a radio programme or to make a comment, your decision will often be based on your desire

• to put forward a point of view;
• to underline that people should continue to pursue a certain line of behaviour;
• to suggest discontinuing a behaviour as in motoring or dietary disciplines.

This means that you are trying to sell an idea or to convince your listeners. The techniques of putting across your ideas are discussed in Unit 3, *Presently Your Case*. Here I want to emphasise three points that will help you to put over your case to your listeners:

1 attention   Start by **talking** about the **listener** and you gain the listener's attention.
2 interest   **Involve** the listener and you will gain the listener's interest
3 action   Aim to **finish with a powerful point** or a request for listener action, for example, 'This is what you should do if you want to take full advantage of this new local development'.

SELF-PREPARATION FOR A RADIO INTERVIEW

The techniques for both radio and television are basically the same, but there are some important differences to bear in mind.

Have a clear communication objective.

CLEAR OBJECTIVES

■ What do you want your listener to know?
■ What do you want your listener to believe?
■ If relevant, what do you want your listener to do?

Stick to two, and never more than three, key points to put over. If you choose three points and there is one above all else that you want to be remembered, put this one last. Listeners tend to hear the first and last things that are said to them.

THREE POINTS ONLY

Use anecdotes, or short vivid stories illustrating success or failure. They are vital ingredients to convey and achieve understanding with your unseen audience. Create simple, easily understood word pictures because a 'picture is worth a thousand words', for example,

tip of the iceberg
as tall as the Eiffel Tower in Paris
pulling the wool over their eyes.

Paint verbal pictures in place of the visuals you would show your listener if you could do so. For instance, if you were trying to explain to your listeners what an asthma attack is:

HELP YOUR LISTENERS
RELATE TO YOUR MESSAGE

> *An asthma attack is rather like the constriction in the flow of water that would result from squeezing a hose pipe. The human equivalent is the windpipe.*

or trying to convey the pleasure of buying fresh fish:

> *When I was a small boy, living at Felpham in Sussex, we always knew that the mackerel brought round on the fish cart was fresh because it had sand on it from the nets being dragged up on the beach from the fishing boat by old Boniface the fisherman and his sons.*

or:

> *Gout is like the rusting up of the joints.*

Since radio is so much simpler than television, it is tempting to respond to an invitation to give your views on the spot to a caller from the radio station, especially if asked, 'Could you give me your opinion on this issue now, because we are going on the air later today?' Always say, 'No, I cannot do it now, can I call you back in about 30 minutes?'. Buy time to consult others as well as time to think about what you are going to say.

 REHEARSE

Rehearse what you are going to say and, just as importantly, how you are going to say it. There is no thinking time on radio as long silences are unacceptable.

Do a dummy run using a colleague to listen to you. Record it on a tape recorder and then you can both critique it.

Know the length of an interview and prepare for it working within the time limits. Never assume that you will be given more time.

HANDLING THE RADIO INTERVIEW

Unlike its television counterpart, the radio studio is much smaller so try to sit with your back to the operations or recording room so that you are not distracted during the recording by the activities going on there.

VERBAL BEHAVIOUR

 AVOID DISTRACTIONS

 AVOID PAUSES

Avoid long pauses. You have no thinking time on radio and, unlike television, there are no picture shots to take up the viewer's attention whilst you collect your ideas.

Like a television interview, you will be asked to do a voice test.

Speak at a sustained volume throughout the radio interview. Modern technology means that the microphone into which you speak is so powerful that you do not need to raise your voice. Even so, do not move about in your chair or turn away from the microphone if a table-mounted or suspended one is used.

Face and speak to the microphone all the time.

Speak clearly, maintain your pitch and remember not to fade at the end of each sentence (see figure 6.1, the 'English fade'). Speak distinctly and not too fast. The listeners have no visual clues so the whole message is received through hearing only.

Although for radio you will not be seen, sit forward in your chair throughout the interview as for a television interview. It will keep you alert and bring alertness to what you say.

SINCERITY AND ENTHUSIASM

You have only one means of communicating on radio – through your voice. So you have to convey everything you think and feel through it.

Be enthusiastic. It comes over to listeners. In any case, if you are not enthusiastic, you should not be doing the interview or taking part in the radio programme at all.

BE ENTHUSIASTIC

Sound interested. Do not attempt to talk about anything you don't believe or don't know about.

Remember, that although you yourself may have heard your comments many times before, for the listener it is new, so put it over with enthusiasm.

Vary your tone and vary the length and pace of your words and sentences.

TYPES OF RADIO INTERVIEW

These are the same as for television, but obviously without the vision:

1 Face-to-face

You and the interviewer discuss an issue. Just to remind you, try to avoid sitting facing the recording room and the operators. Better always to have your back to it to decrease distractions.

2 Panel

This usually involves a group of experts or a group of people who disagree with each other about a specific topic or issue and have been brought together to spark each other off. Here you have to speak up and speak out when you want to make a point as there will be no director giving equal air opportunity to all the panelists. It is worthwhile listening in to some of these types of radio programme to get the feel of how people talk, butt in and make their views heard.

3 Down-the-line

This is where you are picked up, often in a geographic area far distant from the radio station, in a radio car and asked to comment or respond to questions raised by other, equally disembodied and isolated programme participants or interviewers. In such situations, you need to have a well-prepared brief to cling on to so you can use your voice to express clearly and firmly the points you want to make. Sometimes you have to butt in to make a point otherwise you may be overlooked or even forgotten on a panel or down-the-line.

4 Telephone

This is one of the most convenient ways of being interviewed; you are usually on your own territory, at your own desk. You need to handle such requests for interviews so that you have ample time to prepare yourself. Always tell the caller that you will call back in five minutes rather than answer immediately. Stall by saying that you are in a rather noisy office and need to find a quieter one in which to speak to him.

Sometimes the radio station will press you to speak to them immediately. Be firm with such requests let them compromise instead of you. They may have deadlines to meet but so have you.

Then use the time you have bought to think about the subject the radio wants to discuss with you. If possible consult others in your organisation.

Build goodwill with the journalist or interviewer who telephones you. Always promise to ring back within five minutes with your answer rather than giving a blunt refusal without thought.

NOTES

AVOID DISTRACTIONS

Prepare yourself with large printed stab headings on a reminder pad.

Make sure that the office from which you are going to call back and speak to the radio interviewer is a quiet one where you will not be interrupted by incoming telephone calls or other people.

Do not bellow down the telephone. Lift your voice just above normal speaking, slow down and pronounce each word and sentence clearly and crisply.

Do not have a switched on radio in the same room in which you are making the telephone interview or in one next to it, because it will transmit its own signal down the telephone and so back over the air.

5   Outside interviews

These can be out in the open, at a luncheon table, in a motor car whilst driving or being driven, or in a railway carriage. Some producers like them because they add a touch of realism and immediacy to the broadcast.

Unless sound effects like traffic, or aircraft flying

overhead are desired, try to avoid distracting noises. You could end up with everything you planned to say being rendered almost inaudible; then what is the point of going to the trouble of doing the interview?

Remember that all such interviews are likely to be recorded and edited before being broadcast. So, if there are likely to be any comments of yours which could be cut or totally misunderstood, insist on a live studio interview.

Five tips for radio interviews

**C
H
E
C
K
L
I
S
T**

1 Write down the words you are going to start with and know them so that you then just have to glance at the stab printed headings.

2 Prepare the structure of what you are going to say. Think through the mind of the interviewer and imagine what questions you would ask yourself?

3 If necessary, use delaying tactics before answering a question, for example, put questions back to the interviewer such as, 'Bearing in mind the subject we are discussing, why are you asking me that question?'
   When he was Minister of Transport in Mrs Thatcher's Cabinet, Mr Paul Channon was interviewed about a rail strike that was about to start. During the course of the discussion, the interviewer suddenly asked him apropos nothing related to the previous question, 'What is your future in the next Cabinet reshuffle?'

4 If you find yourself in a muddle, don't hesitate to say, 'let me start again'.
   On pre-recorded programmes, if you make a mistake during the recording or get a fact wrong, do not be afraid to say so. Say, 'I'm sorry, I have fluffed that; can we do that bit again please'.

5 If you feel you have discussed a particular subject for long enough do not be afraid to change the area of discussion.

9

Guidelines for Radio and Television Interviews

LEGAL GUIDELINES FOR RADIO AND TELEVISION INTERVIEWS   122

SIR ROBIN DAY'S CODE FOR TELEVISION INTERVIEWERS   122

FOURTEEN WAYS TO DEAL WITH THE PRESS   123

TALKING TO REPORTERS – A GLOSSARY OF TERMS   125

FINAL 'WARNING TO THE WISE' CHECKLIST   127

COMPLAINTS PROCEDURE   128

LEGAL GUIDELINES FOR RADIO AND TELEVISION INTERVIEWS

Most of us have developed a kind of love-hate relationship with the media coloured by first-hand experience or prejudice and based on our religious, political or other views. Programme makers work within specified guidelines laid down by the BBC and the Independent Broadcasting Authority (IBA). Three important features of these guidelines are:

1 Whether the interview is recorded or live, interviewees should be made aware of the format, subject matter and purpose of the programme, as well as the way in which their contribution will be used. Interviewees should also be told the identity and intended role of any other proposed participants in the programme.

2 Interviewees should be told if an edited version of their interview will be shorter and the programme makers should take care that the shortened version does not misrepresent the interviewee's contribution.

3 The context in which extracts from a recorded interview is used is also covered. An interview should not be edited so that, by juxtaposition, a contributor is associated with a line of argument which he or she would probably not accept and have no opportunity to comment on. Neither should separately recorded interviews be edited together so as to give the impression that the contributors are in actual conversation with each other.

SIR ROBIN DAY'S CODE FOR TELEVISION INTERVIEWERS

After years of experience as a television interviewer, he has kindly given permission to reproduce his Code here. It was originally published in 1961 and proudly reprinted in his memoirs in 1989:

1 The television interviewer must do his duty as a journalist, probing for facts and opinions.

2 He should set his own prejudices aside and put questions which reflect various opinions, disregarding probable accusations of bias.

3 He should not allow himself to be overawed in the

presence of a powerful person.

4 He should not compromise the honesty of the interview by omitting awkward topics or by rigging questions in advance.

5 He should resist any inclination in those employing him to soften or rig an interview so as to secure a prestige appearance, or to please authority; if after making his protest the interviewer feels he cannot honestly accept the arrangements, he should withdraw.

6 He should not submit his questions in advance, but it is reasonable to state the main areas of questioning. If he submits specific questions beforehand he is powerless to put any supplementary questions which may be vitally needed to clarify or challenge an answer.

7 He should give fair opportunity to answer questions, subject to the time limits imposed by television.

8 He should never take advantage of his professional experience to trap or embarrass someone unused to television appearances.

9 He should press his questions firmly and persistently, but not tediously, offensively or merely in order to sound tough.

10 He should remember that a television interviewer is not employed as a debater, prosecutor, inquisitor, psychiatrist or third-degree expert, but as a journalist seeking information on behalf of the viewer.

FOURTEEN WAYS TO DEAL WITH THE PRESS

In an article on managing, *Fortune* magazine in June 1989 said that declaring war on the press, tempting as it may sometimes be, is a game you cannot win. Then it listed the following guidelines*:

1 Make the chief executive officer responsible for press relations

This means the officer must often speak for the corporation, both routinely and in times of crisis, and delegate enough authority to make the public relations spokesman a credible source.

* Reprinted by kind permission of *Fortune Magazine*, © The Time Inc. Magazine Company, 1989.

2 Face the facts

If you screw up, admit it candidly. Avoid hedging or excuses. Apologise, promise not to do it again, and explain how you are going to make things right.

3 Consider the public interest in every operating decision.

Your reputation depends far more on what you do than on what you say. Act accordingly. Try giving your senior public relations expert a seat at the table when decisions are made.

4 Be a source before you are a subject.

The time to make friends with reporters is long before trouble hits. Get to know the people who cover your company, educate them, help them with their stories and give them reason to respect you. Determine which journalists deserve your respect and trust.

5 If you want your views represented, you have to talk.

Reporters are paid to get stories, whether you help or not. When you clam up, they must depend on other sources — often people like that marketing vice-president you fired last month.

6 Respond fast.

You cannot influence a story once its deadline has passed. Nor will you appear credible if you seem to be stalling. In a crisis, figure you have a day to get your story out.

7 Cage your lawyers.

They will always tell you to keep your mouth shut. However, in many crisis situations your potential legal liability may be trivial compared with the risk of alienating your customers, employees, or regulators.

8 Tell the truth – or nothing.

Nobody likes a liar.

9 Don't expect to bat 1,000.

Public relations is a game of averages, so be content if you win most of the time. Even the most flattering story will likely have a *zinger* or two, and even the best companies get creamed now and then.

10 Don't take it personally.

The reporter is neither your enemy nor your friend: he or she is an intermediary between you and the people you need to reach. Forget about your ego; nobody cares about it but you.

11 Control what you can.

Release the bad news yourself before some reporter digs it up. Use your selective availability to reporters as a tool. Set ground rules every time you talk. If the public isn't buying your message, change it.

12 Know who you are dealing with.

The press is not monolithic. Television is different from print, magazines are different from newspapers and the *Austin-Statesman* is different from the *Wall Street Journal*. Within a news organisation there will be a normal mix of individuals, some honourable and competent, some not. Do your homework on journalists before you talk to them, reviewing their past work and talking to other executives they have covered.

13 Avoid television unless you feel free to speak candidly. Even then, learn to present your views in the ten-second sound bites that are the building blocks of television stories. Use simple, declarative sentences and ignore subtleties. Whenever possible favour live television shows over those that can edit your remarks.

14 Be human.

The public will usually be more sympathetic to a person than to a corporation. If you can do it without lying or making a fool of yourself, reveal yourself as a person with feelings. Your mistakes will as likely be forgiven as criticised. Insist on being judged on a human scale, with normal human fallibility taken into account. Remember that people love to root for underdogs.

In the same article, *Fortune* set out a short glossary for talking to reporters. Here it is.

TALKING TO REPORTERS – A GLOSSARY OF TERMS

Negotiate the ground rules with reporters before you volunteer information. Knowing these definitions will help you.

1 Off the record.

Material may not be published or broadcast, period. Do not go off the record casually or with anyone you do not have reason to trust.

2 Not for attribution.

Information may be published, but without revealing the identity of the source.

Always specify whether that applies to your company as well as to yourself. Nail down the attribution the reporter will use – 'A member of Acme Corp's two-man executive committee' versus 'an industry expert' – before you open your mouth.

3 Background.

Usually means material not for attribution. Do not take this for granted. Discuss it with the reporter.

4 Deep background.

Usually means off the record.

Again, make sure.

5 Just between us.

And other ambiguous phrases mean little to reporters. Do not use them.

6 Check it with me before you use it.

Means just what it says.

Specify whether the restriction applies to quotations as well as facts. When the reporter checks back, you have the right to correct errors and misunderstandings, but not to withdraw statements you now regret.

7 Read it to me before you use it.

Gives you no right even to correct errors. All you get is advance warning of what the reporter will use.

8 No.

Means that you have decided not to answer a reporter's question.

Used judiciously, this can be a life saver.

This article signs off with the following wise words:

> 'The bottom line, which is not exactly news, is that dealing with the press means dealing with perception. That may be uncomfortable for executives used to communicating hard facts. Certainly trying to convey perceptions through the filters of reporters, editors and producers is risky. But it is less risky, on balance, than not trying'.

FINAL 'WARNING TO THE WISE' CHECKLIST

The best way to avoid unpleasantness or arguments with the media and having to resort to the complaints department of the broadcasting authorities, or worse still the law, is to follow a few sensible rules.

C H E C K L I S T	**Warnings to the wise**
	■ Get it right in the first place what your involvement is going to be in any interview or programme.
	■ Brief yourself and others in your organisation (who you are consulting) on your involvement in order to avoid possible pitfalls.
	■ Before it takes place, establish what type of programme you have been invited to contribute to or participate in?
	■ Get as many details about it as possible.
	■ Obtain confirmation that none of your comments will be used in a repeat programme or out of context without obtaining your prior permission.
	■ Know your rights as defined by the BBC and IBA guidelines.
	■ If you or any part of your organisation is to be filmed, make sure that the film crew is accompanied throughout any visit(s) by a senior member of your company. This person must be briefed about the purpose of the filming, the objectives, any no go areas, or questions that might be asked by the film crew.
	■ During the filming, make sure that you are clear and precise in dealing with questions. Be as short in your replies as possible. Beware of how your answers could be edited.

COMPLAINTS PROCEDURE

If you are unhappy with the way you have been treated by a programme on which you have appeared, discuss it with your management colleagues and, if there is one, the head of your public relations.

Then, if still not satisfied, you should complain first to the Director General of the BBC or IBA and then to the Broadcasting Complaints Commission whose address is:
Grosvenor Gardens House
35 & 37 Grosvenor Gardens
London SW1W 0BS.

Viewers or listeners who have a complaint which they wish the Commission to consider should write to the Secretary to the Commission giving the title of the relevant programme and the date and channel on which it was broadcast. They should explain in what way they consider that the programme was unjust or unfair, or in what way they consider that their privacy was unwarrantably infringed. If they were not a participant in the programme, they should also explain in what way they consider that they have some degree of direct interest.

When the Commission have considered and adjudicated upon a complaint, copies of their adjudication and a summary of it are sent at the same time to the complainant and the broadcasters. It is the Commission's normal practice, whether or not the complaint has been upheld, to direct the broadcasters to broadcast the summary and to publish it in the Radio or TV Times as appropriate. The summary of the Commission's adjudication is usually broadcast on the same channel as and at a similar time to the programme which was the subject of the complaint. This is the only sanction available to the Commission; they cannot require the broadcasters to apologoise to the complainant, to broadcast a correction or to provide a financial remedy.

If all else fails, as a last resort take legal action quickly, using a lawyer with specialist experience in media litigation so that he does not have to go through a long learning curve at your expense.

10

The Press

CONVENTION IN HANDLING THE PRESS   131

HOW TO AVOID MISREPRESENTATION   132

FEATURES FOR PUBLICATION   134

ON *THE RECORD* REAL LIFE CASE STUDIES   138

COMPLAINTS PROCEDURE   144

FACING THE PRESS   145

When dealing with the press, either for an article or in response to a request for an opinion, it is important to understand clearly the uses to which the information you provide may be put.

The aims and interests of journalists and those of your company or organisation do not usually coincide. A journalist's first loyalty is always to his or her readers, not to his or her sources of information. Conversely, your first loyalty is to your company or organisation and its reputation.

Beware of making assumptions about the motives of others. You may be motivated by money. A great many journalists are not. Their ambitions are often quaint and complex. The search for the truth and exposing it can be a compelling drug for many.

Journalists are a part of the hard-nosed business of publishing. Remember that when you meet a young, and perhaps to you humbly paid, man or woman, the journalist is always in control. It is what they report back to their publications that gets into print.

Always clarify with journalists how the information you provide will be used. You must draw a line between *supplying* information and *using* information as a means of winning the journalist's loyalty to your cause. If journalists forget to whom they owe their first loyalty, the price could be their job.

Beware of freelance journalists who ring you up and ask for an interview. Often they have no status and are hoping that you may be able to give them sufficient hot or juicy information around which they will be able to write a saleable article. Always ask such journalists to show you written confirmation of the article they have been commissioned to write, the name of the publication in which it is to appear and the date when it will be published.

It is better to supply information that clarifies a situation to journalists than to refuse to do so. This prevents them stating that when the company in question was invited to make a statement, it refused to comment on the allegations. This type of remark can only sow seeds of doubt and suspicion in the minds of readers or viewers that you have something to hide.

CONVENTION IN HANDLING THE PRESS

When you talk to the press, there are a number of conventions about how what you say may be reported. Always clarify before any interview takes place, the basis upon which you are prepared to be interviewed.

Anything you say 'on the record' may be attributed to you as a direct quotation.

ON THE RECORD

Unless you deal with this matter clearly and firmly before the interview starts, then the journalist will **assume that everything is on the record**. After such an interview, the journalist is at liberty to use any information you gave him without clearing it with you first.

Implications of on the record interviews include the following points:

- You have no automatic right to a preview of any written material in which you are quoted, although you should always ask anyway.
- If, in an on the record interview you prefer not to be named in person, tell the journalist that whilst anything you say is on the record, you wish it to be attributed to a company spokesperson and not to you by name.
- Sometimes you may want to give a journalist some background information, the better to understand what your about to say. Then, state that you wish to offer an **unattributable view** which is not to be quoted, nor attributed to you.
- If you do not wish to be quoted at all, but are willing for the information you provide to be incorporated in an article, tell the journalist that you are **speaking unattributably** (see page 112).

Never, never speak to a journalist 'off the record'. If you want to be sure that something remains off the record do not tell it to a journalist. You cannot attempt to collude with someone whose loyalties, aims and motivations are different from yours.

OFF THE RECORD

HOW TO AVOID MISREPRESENTATION

Although there is always a risk of being misrepresented by the press, this danger can be minimised by bearing these points in mind.

✓ STICK TO THE FACTS

BE ACCURATE

Always ensure that what you say is accurate and as straightforwardly factual as possible. Facts can be verified, opinions cannot be.

If you are asked a factual question to which you do not know the answer, do not hesitate to say so. If the question is an important one for your organisation then add that you will do your best to find out.

USING A TAPE RECORDER

Some journalists prefer to conduct an on the record interview using a tape recorder rather than taking down your comments in shorthand.

Clarify the basis on which the tape will be used, although as a rule there is no reason why you should object.

When a journalist uses a tape recorder for an interview, some interviewees feel that they should get their own tape recorders out and make a separate recording of the conversation. Whilst a journalist probably will not object, it does not help the two-way flow of the interview.

COMPLEX INFORMATION

If your interview with a journalist is likely to involve reference to figures or complex, dificult facts, it is best to send such information in advance of the interview. Always spell out unusual or unfamiliar words.

DON'T FEAR SILENCE

During a interview there may be pauses whilst the journalist is framing the next question. Do not let the silence bother you. It is the interviewer's problem, not yours. Make the statement you want to make or answer the question as you planned and then **stop talking** and **wait** for the next question.

✓ STOP TALKING

COMPLAINING ABOUT WHAT IS PRINTED

If, following an interview on the record, you complain that you have been misquoted, the journalist may play back the transcript and prove that you did say what you now dispute. At this point, it is no good saying, 'Well that's all very well, but what I meant to say was . . .'.

When speaking to a journalist on the record, beware when he closes his notebook as he prepares to leave. You inwardly give a sigh of relief and may let your cautious behaviour relax. This is when so many interviewees make the most damaging and quotable comments.

If you become incensed by something that has been printed about you or your company, declaring war on the press is one fight that you will never win, be you ever so powerful or rich.

DO NOT WAGE WAR AGAINST THE PRESS

If a journalist is working to a deadline, find out what this is. If it is too close for you to be able to obtain the necessary answers to the questions raised, say 'I'm sorry, I won't be able to get back to you before that time. Would you still like me to find out?'.

PRESS DEADLINES

Even if you are pressed, never speculate under pressure. If the journalist still presses and asks you to speculate, by prompts such as, 'Well do you think that such and such is probably the case?', decline to answer or even to indicate that you agree with this line of argument.

DON'T SPECULATE

Her Majesty's Press. Do not be conned by journalists who try and put over the importance of their job as guardians of the public's conscience or who say that the people have a right to know what's going on.

Few journalists know what they are talking about or what they are planning to write about. Their skill is in being able to collect the facts and then write them down in cogent and attractive language that people will want to read.

ENSURE UNDERSTANDING

Journalists need educating. So, when imparting information, ensure that he or she has fully understood what you have said. Test their understanding of what you have told them by getting them to feedback what you have said.

TEST UNDERSTANDING

If you do not feel confident that you understand something that a journalist wants to discuss with you, be careful. Preferably do not discuss it. Answering a journalist's query with a statement which you do not fully understand will probably be detected by the person to whom you are speaking and this could undermine the rest of the interview.

ADMIT IGNORANCE

If you are faced with this problem, admit to the journalist that he or she is asking about an area you do not understand. Offer to find someone with the specialist knowledge required who can call the journalist back and explain it competently. To ensure that you are clear in the brief you provide a colleague, ask the journalist to let you have his or her questions clearly so that you can write them down. Be sure to call back all such questions to the journalist to check that you have got them correctly written down.

FEATURES FOR PUBLICATION

The preceding sections of this unit relate mainly to stories appearing in print and describes how you should **react** to approaches made to you by the press. In addition, there is an important **proactive** opportunity which you and your organisation should be ready to exploit to your advantage when the time and the material are right to do so.

You can obtain positive publicity and goodwill for your organisation and its activities from feature articles. Do not look on this as a glorious opening for you to achieve that life ambition to become a writer. An outside expert is rarely asked to write an article for a newspaper or magazine. However, if it does happen do not be fooled into thinking that 2,500 words can be rattled off in a couple of hours. Consider the better option of using a professional journalist to ghost the article for you even if it is expensive.

Usually an article will be written by a journalist, based on an interview and other relevant material supplied by one or more outside experts. A journalist, writing a comparative piece, will want to talk to sources other than you and quite probably, if you are a commercial company, to some of your competitors. From whatever material you supply, either at an interview or in written form, the journalist will select that which he or she thinks will best meet the reader's needs and expectations. The final copy will also reflect, not only the journalist's own style, but the way in which the commissioning publication likes material to be expressed. Although, the result may not always be to your choice or how you would have written it, remember that the journalist is the expert communicator and you should respect this expertise.

If you give an interview, as I have said many times in this manual, prepare the material and yourself thoroughly. Before granting a journalist an interview, it is worthwhile asking yourself whether it will be beneficial to do so. Do not be flattered by the invitation, especially if it is the first time this has happened to you. Ask yourself the following questions:

1 Does the article this journalist is proposing to write sound interesting?

If the topic proposed is say, *Opportunities for computer programmers in engineering*, or whatever your particular specialist business is, **BEWARE**. The idea may well have been thought up to fit the space between the advertisements in the computer vacancies section of the magazine or newspaper. Always be on your guard against public relations puffs used to separate advertisements. I have been asked to write for marketing magazines whose annual calendar is built around such topics as *Conference and exhibitions*, *Sales incentives and promotions* and *Marketing research*. When you analyse the articles that appear each month, they contain one or more relating to the specialist marketing activity for which they hope to sell advertising space. The *Financial Times* weekly and monthly supplements have been built around this strategy. Unless you want to attract computer programmers or whatever the particular specialist jobs being featured are, it is not worth cooperating with the publication.

2 Does the journalist appear to know anything about the subject?

Despite what I have said previously, some journalists specialise and become deeply knowledgeable about a particular industry or activity. One or two pointed questions about how he or she plans to tackle the subject will soon indicate the depth of knowledge or ignorance.

Do remember that knowing nothing about a subject does not necessarily disqualify a journalist from writing a good article about it. However, it does mean that those who are interviewed need to take great care with how they impart information and beware of the dangers of using specialist jargon. The journalist might not understand but may refrain from admitting ignorance.

I recall an occasion when I was one of a number of experts interviewed by a freelance journalist about the pharmaceutical industry. She decided to send me the draft of the whole article she proposed to send in to the publication in which it would be printed. Some of the people she had interviewed had given her information which anyone in the industry would spot at once as wrong if it had been reproduced as she had written it. Fortunately, she accepted my advice on matters of fact, re-checked them and made corrections to the copy before it went to press.

USE OF TAPE RECORDERS

For an article interview, if the journalist wishes to use a tape recorder, allow it unless there is a particular reason for objecting. Sadly, few journalists now write in shorthand so tape recorders are an essential part of a journalist's equipment.

For articles of a highly complex or technical nature, you may also wish to have a tape recorder handy so that you can record the interview.

If you are concerned about the danger of being misrepresented, ask someone else in your organisation to sit in on the interview.

TELEPHONE INTERVIEWS

For feature articles, face-to-face interviews are better than telephone conversations. If the deadline is short for the article, you may have no alternative but to give an interview by telephone.

Be careful about talking *off the cuff* on highly sensitive or political issues. Where time allows, always call the journalist back after you have had time to think about the subject and what your responses would be to potential questions.

As a general rule, it is wise to give a telephone interview for an article only if the subject matter is straightforward and the interview itself is likely to be short.

FACE-TO-FACE INTERVIEWS

If the subject matter is complex and the journalist is to interview you in person, see whether you can arrange to have some published material available. This can be taken away and studied and may also serve to draw attention to the correct spellings of unusual or highly scientific words.

Here your preparation for the interview should include thinking about what documentation might help the journalist. Consider your company's annual report, reprints of articles, scientific or specialist papers presented to a conference, the organisation's public relations files and cuttings books. All these should be to hand, with photocopies ready if you plan to give the journalist any of the material to take away.

Journalists work to different deadlines, according to the frequency of the publication for which they are writing. There is nearly always more time available for preparation of feature material than there is for news copy for publications like a national daily that has to be *put to bed* by 7.00 pm on the day before publication. Consequently, you should always confirm in advance of granting an interview, that you will either be shown or read what the journalist writes about you or your organisation before it is published. It is best if you can actually see the text. If time is too short for this, the journalist should agree to call you back when the article is finished and read over what he has written.

PREVIEWING MATERIAL

If you have an opportunity to comment, restrict yourself to matters of fact relating to your own interview and what you said. It is unlikely that a journalist would read the other sections of his article over to you but, if this happens, you have no right to criticise them, still less to change them. Similarly, if the journalist has expressed an opinion with which you disagree, that is his or her perogative. On the other hand, if you feel that the opinion expressed by the journalist is based on a misunderstanding of the facts as you gave them, then point this out firmly but quietly. If you communicate that you are annoyed or angry about a specific item, you could provide the journalist with ammunition to strengthen a slant given to that section of the article which bears upon your interview. Only insist on a change if there is clearly a factual error, or if you have been quoted as saying something you did not say. Remember that you have no right to withdraw something which you did say but, on reflection, wish you had not expressed. Perhaps it was said during one of those journalistic silences which you filled with thoughtless, but nevertheless, damaging thoughts.

If you are sent an article in draft form and it includes comments from a variety of sources, some of them perhaps made by your competitors about you, you have no right to request a change to the text unless what is said is wrong and you can prove it to be so. You may not like the views expressed in the article by other people, but that is the price we all pay for a free press. You should, however, not hesitate to point out any errors of fact in parts of the article not concerned with what you said and suggest to the journalist that he checks them with the source(s) from which they were obtained.

Sometimes, despite all the checks and references back to you about copy, the article that appears or that part of it that refers to your interview, is wrong. Do not jump to the conclusion that it was the journalist's fault. The story may have been changed, cut or reworded by a sub-editor.

Finally, if you are unhappy with what appears in print, try not to take it too seriously. Newspapers are largely ephemeral, their contents soon forgotten by most people before the next issue comes out. Only if damaging untruths or misinterpretations are printed should you try to seek redress. Otherwise, it is always salutary to remember that today's newspaper lights tomorrow's bonfire.

ON THE RECORD REAL LIFE CASE STUDIES

The following three case studies provide an ominous warning that even well-known people, with a multitude of professional advice at their disposal, can make some basic mistakes in their *on their record* dealings with the press.

CASE STUDY ONE:

Nick Faldo, international golfer and others
'*Never sweet talk to a stranger*'*

* Reprinted by kind permission of Joe Joseph from an article he wrote for The (London) Times on April 11th 1991. * The Times, 1991. All rights reserved.

Would-be celebrities, who chat to journalists, wake up, skim the morning newspapers and discover that they have become just a little more celebrated than they had planned, have a habit of complaining that they have been 'stitched up'. They rarely acknowledge that they have provided the needle and thread.

I am not talking about journalists who quote something spicy they have gleaned from a friend of the Princess of Wales. I am talking about journalists who write stories after having been invited to someone's home for the chance to get a long, cosy look at the subject. They do not break down the door. They have been invited in. Many are begged. Why do grown people, many of whom should know better, do it?

The latest moaner is the golfer Nick Faldo. Many interviewees, when they see their words in print, cannot believe they speak so inelegantly and with so little anecdotal spark. The wise (or cruel?) interviewer is always ready to play back a tape and to wait for the inevitable, 'Well I said it, but that's not what I meant'.

What exactly does someone like Nick Faldo mean? His pushy personal agent, worried that his client was rated in America as a cracking golfer but not a cuddly one, arranged for a reporter from *Sport Illustrated*, a pukkah sports magazine, to spend a week with Faldo in Australia. The interview has just been published in America and done for the 19th hole chit-chat what Kitty Kelley's biography of Nancy Reagan is doing at the moment for Georgetown dinner parties.

Sports Illustrated was hardly snooping on Faldo, who, in the course of a week, made several unflattering remarks about his top rivals. He questioned the proficiency of Paul Azinger ('bad technique') and of Greg Norman ('his swing . . . it's way too loose'), as well as Payne Stewart's dress sense and the demeanour of Curtis Strange.

Faldo, reaching for the thesaurus of aggrieved interviewees, said, 'This is going to cause me embarrassment. And I can do without it. I'll just tell the guys "Sorry, but I've been stitched up"'.

What did Faldo and his agent think they were doing inviting a journalist to spend seven days as his Siamese twin? After a week of such intimacy most married couples would learn enough about each other to demand a divorce. *Sports Illustrated* was not writing a book, just a magazine article. Faldo only had to make a couple of unguarded comments every 24 hours to make his new companion's trip to Australia worthwhile.

As it was, Faldo could not bear to read more than the first paragraph of the piece, which began, 'Why does Faldo have to be like this? Why does he have to be this mechanical man with the wrinkle-proof sweater, the smile-proof mouth and the 75%-proof swing? What is it that makes him want to be the world's most impeccable grouch? . . . Every time Faldo says 'nice shot' to somebody, they put up another pyramid in Egypt'.

Oh dear, Nick, join the queue and pass the thesaurus. Ian Botham has already thumbed through it several times. So has Nicholas Ridley (a Tory Member of Parliament and Secretary of State for the Department of Trade and Industry in Margaret Thatcher's last Cabinet from 1987 to November 1990), after being hurtful about Helmut Kohl in an interview with the *Spectator*: 'I deeply resent the journal's assumption that I associate present day Germany with the aggression of the past,' he whined, 'I don't hold that view'.

A big part of the problem is that many people are vain, many others greedy. Quite a few are both. Journalists are often asked by friends who have just received a request for an interview whether they should accept. Most journalists do not blink before replying, 'Lock your doors. Disconnect your phone. You have little to gain, possibly a great deal to lose'. Do they listen? People will stay up till dawn waiting for the paper to flop on to the doormat so they can see their faces and read their words, however humdrum.

If Faldo didn't yearn for the financial rewards of being loved by American housewives, if Nicholas Ridley did not believe his views on Europe so vital that they must be shared with the nation, they would still be happy men. It is not very difficult to keep your trap shut. The Queen and the Queen Mother have been doing it for years. So has John Profumo. Greta Garbo never talked. Jacqueline Onassis won't discuss Dallas, 1963. Denis Thatcher remains discreet.

Gerald Ratner pays price for cheap publicity

Gerald Ratner, is the chairman of the 238-strong jewellery chain that bears his name. On April 23 1991, he had been invited to make one of the keynote speeches at the annual convention of The Institute of Directors (IOD), held at The Albert Hall, London. I had been invited to attend it as a member of the press and was sitting just below the speakers' platform.

Gerald Ratner was the last to speak in the afternoon following the traditional luncheon box feast provided to all delegates. So he had to contend with one of a speaker's most awesome challenges – how to keep delegates awake and listening. Conscious of this problem, Ratner once or twice departed from his prepared speech to make some off the cuff asides which he hoped would hold the attention of the audience. He referred to some of the products in his outlets as 'total crap'. This did not appear in the press handout of his speech of which I had a copy.

Following this conference speech, sales nose-dived and he was forced to launch an advertising campaign, estimated to have cost the group between £250,000 and £500,000 to try and offset the effects of his much publicised comments that some of his merchandise was cheap and tacky. Outside the Christmas season, this retail group had never previously advertised in the national press. On May 23 the advertising and promotion magazine, *Campaign* reported that 'sales slumped despite a desperate celebrity-endorsing ad campaign rushed out the following week [after the April IOD Convention]'.

This is a sad example of self-induced press damage brought about by lack of thought of the dangers that off the cuff remarks can produce. They may have been aimed at galvanising the audience, but for the press they were considered to be ill-judged and flippant. And the stories they filed showed this only too plainly.

CASE STUDY THREE: **Thatcher and 'home' – the** *Vanity Fair* **interview**

In May 1991, the world's press and television programmes carried the story of the former British Prime Minister, Margaret Thatcher's interview with Maureen Orth which was printed in the *Vanity Fair* magazine.

The London Daily Telegraph carried the front page headline: 'Thatcher shattered by her speedy exit' above the summary of the interview she had given in Washington to the *Vanity Fair* magazine. As Bill Deedes wrote in his *Personal View* column on June 6, 1991:*

'It was fair comment, but not a phrase to linger long in people's minds. The phrase that lingered and was much discussed came in our second headline taken from the interview, 'Home is where you come to when you have nothing better to do'.

Reactions were swift. Letters appeared in many newspapers (including this one) pointing out that upwards of two million unemployed had nowhere else to go but home, and criticising Mrs Thatcher for snivelling about it. The phrase made a field day for those who cordially dislike her.

Mrs Thatcher, though deeply hurt, made no public comment. There existed, however, an independent tape of the interview and a second version of Mrs Thatcher's fateful words appeared in *The Times* of May 24 1991. At this point in the interview she was discussing her family. The sentence as spoken ran on these lines: 'And sometimes if something happens and we don't see the family as often as we would wish, and they go off I say: "Well, look, home is where you come to when you haven't anything better to do. We are always there"'.

Paul Johnson took it up in *The Spectator* of June 1, concluding that *Vanity Fair* was 'guilty of an infamous piece of journalistic misconduct'. Love of home and family, he rightly pointed out, is one of Mrs Thatcher's strongest emotions. The disputed passage in the *Vanity Fair* interview conveyed precisely the opposite impression. I commented in my column: 'Accidental, I suppose, but are we sure?'

The effect of all this was to draw the badger. On June 4 a lengthy letter appeared in *The Times* from Tina Brown, editor-in-chief of *Vanity Fair*, defending the interview. To call the letter disingenuous would be charitable. 'Whoever released the transcript of her interview with *Vanity Fair*', she wrote, 'has chosen to punctuate these words and those surrounding them in such a way that they read as an exhortation to her children. But the tricky business of punctuating spoken remarks without the nuances of voice and expression should not be allowed to obscure the main issue'.

Mrs Thatcher's remark was not in any way extraordinary. On the contrary, it was commonplace, being what many parents are moved lightly but lovingly to say to children who grow older and move away: Your home is always here, and when you have nothing better to do come back to it, because we are always here to welcome you. That was what Mrs Thatcher said, and what people who know her would expect her to say. What she was made to say by *Vanity Fair*, which highlighted the sentence in its promotional material, was a travesty, though not one which a great many people have noticed. People are careless about injustices towards those they have no liking for, and the reaction of many of Mrs Thatcher's detractors will be to shrug and say that she was foolish to give the interview in the first place.

But I think that we must be more particular than that. 'Modern communications corrupt good manners', Anthony Eden once observed when he was Foreign Secretary, and that is truer now that it was when he said it.

I believe strongly in the value of antagonism between politicians and the media. It gives the discerning citizen, caught between these powerful groups, a chance to use commonsense and to spot the truth of the matter. In any sound democracy these relationships ought to be abrasive. The chief feature of any dictatorship is the demand of the politician that the media should submit to political requirements. But this valuable abrasiveness is destroyed if one side cheats; if, on the one hand, the media resort to untruths about the politician or, on the other, the politician (who has the last word) responds by throwing legislation against the media. To make this arrangement work, both sides must play fair. Oddly, I think this is something Mr Tony Benn, with whom I seldom agree, understands. Rarely without a tape recorder, he is vigilant against cheating. In this respect, he seems to me eminently sane.

In this instance one side did cheat and the rest of us were misled into doing Mrs Thatcher a serious injustice. We looked at what appeared to be an unsual interview with Mrs Thatcher and (naturally) reported the most controversial parts of it. One part was wrong. No matter whether Mrs Thatcher is universally loved or loathed. That has no relevance. Mrs Thatcher was distressed by what appeared, though she made no complaint. We were wrong, and we are sorry'.

CASE STUDIES:
CONCLUSIONS

These three case studies, although about contrasting people and events, bring out some important lessons for anyone who from choice or necessity, has to face the press and be interviewed.

COMPLAINTS PROCEDURE

If you have a complaint about an item in a newspaper which concerns inaccuracy, intrusion, harassment or discrimination, write to the editor about it.

If you are still dissatisfied you can write to the Press Complaints Commission whose address is:
1 Salisbury Square
London EC4Y 8AE

The PCC is an independent organisation charged with enforcing an editorial Code of Practice for the press.

Facing the press

■ Is there a compelling reason for granting or seeking an interview with the media? If there is not, then do not give one.

■ What are the objectives of the interview, both yours and that of the journalist?

■ Never give a press interview without meticulous preparation.

■ From the start to the finish of the interview, answer the questions as you planned to. Make only the statements that you planned to make and then **shut up**. Do not fear the ensuing silence. I suspect that Mrs Thatcher's reported and shortened remarks about the family that caused her so much hurt, were not part of her scripted preparations for the *Vanity Fair* interview. Had she written down such a comment and submitted it to her erstwhile head of press relations at 10 Downing Street, Bernard Ingham, I am sure that he would have spotted the way in which the promotional vultures could and did abbreviate her reply to make sensational copy.

■ If you can, always answer questions in as few words as possible so that editing is difficult, if not impossible.

■ The longer the interview, the greater the danger that you will let your guard down and say something unplanned and damaging. If, for practical reasons, an interview has to extend over a period of two or more hours, arrange to have a break away from the journalist conducting the interview.

■ Know what you are going to say, say it and then shut up.

C
H
E
C
K
L
I
S
T

11

Training Yourself to Face The Press

EXTERNAL WORKSHOPS   147

INDIVIDUAL TUITION   148

AN IN-HOUSE PROGRAMME   149

HOW TO STRUCTURE A COMPANY PROGRAMME   149

COURSE TRAINING OBJECTIVES   150

CONTENT OF WORKSHOPS   151

This manual has been written with the sole purpose of helping you to be more successful in future when, either from choice or necessity, you have to *face the press*.

Some of you, having read this manual, may find it comparatively easy to apply the techniques I have described; but probably the majority will ask, 'How can I be trained to develop my knowledge and skills to face the press effectively?' Some of you may be the managing director of a small company, others may be one of several directors or senior managers of a large firm, a multi-national or public organisation. You can obtain training via the following options.

EXTERNAL WORKSHOPS

For the director or general manager of a small company where it would be expensive, or impractical to have a workshop specially designed for one person, there are a growing number of external courses devoted to the sole objective of training senior personnel how to handle the media.

Here are some guidelines to help you to decide which course you should attend to meet your training needs.

1 Define your own training objective in terms of
   a) What you need to know and understand about the media.
   b) What you must be able to do. For example, do you need to be able to brief journalists at company annual general meetings, issue and be prepared to comment on press releases to the media, be able to handle interviews with the media in person, on radio and television, on the telephone, down-the-line?
   c) What standards of presentation and interviewing skills you must attain to be able to undertake media interviews.

This analysis will help you pinpoint and answer the question of what you must be able to do at the end of the training course.

2 Send for information about these training courses on how to handle the media. Check the following with the

organisers:

a) Who actually conducts the programme? What are their qualifications? They should include having first-hand experience as a journalist, perhaps as someone on the other side of the fence like you, and above all they must have been trained to train.

b) Which companies or organisations have used the course regularly?

c) How many attend each course? Since your objective is to develop yourself, you want to be sure that you will be given a lot of individual tuition. Ideally, there should not be more than six delegates on such a programme, preferably with two tutors and the use of professional radio or television interviewers to put you through simulated press, radio and face-to-face interviews.

d) Ask the course organisers for the names and telephone numbers of at least three people, in positions similar to your own, who have attended the course which you decide best suits your needs and to whom you can speak about the programme and its quality and effectiveness.

INDIVIDUAL TUITION

As an alternative to attending an external programme, you could arrange to have a programme of private tuition from an acknowledged expert just before you are going to have a press, radio or television interview. I have undertaken such tuition for politicians and heads of organisations, especially when they are doing it for the first time and in strange conditions, such as in a foreign country and through an interpreter.

The benefits of such private tuition are

- It can be related to the individual's specific interviewing needs and topics.
- The tutor can help you to script some specifically-tailored statements and carry out *devil's advocate* question and answer sessions on critical topics which you are likely to be faced with by the media.

• Coach you on an individual basis.

The cost of such individual tuition is likely to be high. On the other hand the benefits should more than outweigh the costs, not least because of the fact that it would be built around a very precise interview situation you will be facing immediately afterwards.

AN IN-HOUSE PROGRAMME

A great number of commercial companies, public organisations and associations such as the *Building Societies Association*, the *Institute of Chartered Accountants of England and Wales*, the *Law Society* and the *Royal Institute of British Architects* employ or have sufficiently large memberships to justify designing an in-house training programme.

This can be organised through the central management development or human resources manager or by commissioning a specialist consultant who is an expert in media training.

HOW TO STRUCTURE A COMPANY PROGRAMME

Here are some guidelines on how a *face the press* workshop might be constructed. The term workshop is used deliberately to indicate a learning experience during which systems, techniques and skills would be developed to the point of practical application in situations that are likely to be faced by the delegates at the completion of the workshop.

<table>
<tr><td>C
H
E
C
K
L
I
S
T</td><td>

Course training objectives

By the end of the workshop, delegates should be able to:
- set clear objectives for media interviews and at the same time understand those of the media;
- control media meetings and interviews so that the televised, broadcast or published features do not contain nasty surprises of what was said in an unguarded moment and regretted later;
- handle sensitive issues so that correct facts and impressions are conveyed to the public;
- prepare, structure and conduct all types of media interview.

</td></tr>
</table>

Content of workshops
Based on the objectives above, the material covered would include: ■ Handling the media: an opportunity for delegates to discuss their individual perceptions and firsthand experiences, if any, of dealing with the media. ■ Press, radio and television interviewing: the case for and against doing it; nature and features of press and television interviews; how to prepare and structure such interviews; preparing checklists for such interviews (see unit 5); television studio and outside broadcasts; what to expect; who does what; your appearance and manner. ■ Handling the interview: the rules that apply; key points; self assessment. ■ Radio and telephone interviews: the differences between television and press interviews; how to prepare yourself; types of interview-face-to-face, panel, down-the-line, telephone on to tape, outside. ■ Guidelines governing radio and television interviews. ■ The press: articles for publication; the process and the pitfalls; editing and ability to comment; using tape recorder for interviewing.

C H E C K L I S T

Method: The workshop should be designed to allow the maximum amount of time for discussion and questions arising from each subject after it has been presented and developed by the tutor.

The bulk of the workshop (over 70 per cent) should be allocated to developing media interviewing skills, ideally using all the technical equipment now deployed by radio, television and the press. This will include a television studio with two to three cameras so that delegates can get a lifelike experience of studio conditions, additional rooms with television cameras and recording equipment for individual one-to-one interviews and telephones wired into a tape recorder so that telephone interviews can be recorded and analysed.

If the tutors are not highly skilled in all types of television, radio and press interviews, then you need to retain the services of one, or preferably two, professional interviewers. A number of the men and women who one sees on the BBC and independent television news programmes are freelance and, provided they are given sufficient advance notice, will be willing to undertake such workshop interviewing of delegates. Their fees, depending upon their reputation, range from £250 to £1,000 per day.

Role-playing: The most effective way to develop skill in being interviewed is through repeated practice. To achieve this, each delegate should have to handle a variety of media interviews during the workshop, ideally dealing with subject matters related to his or her field of activity.

These role-plays should include one-to-one interviews with a professional journalist, one-to-one telephone interviews by a journalist seeking material for an article with a tight copy deadline, emergency telephone interviews about a crisis at a chemical plant or about a political scandal for instance. These crisis interview situations should require the delegates to be awoken in the early hours of the morning or to be called out from the middle of a meal. This will test how effectively they can manage such off the cuff requests for comment.

Simulate press conference situations such as company annual general meetings in which all the delegates undertake specific roles or when a special announcement has to be made to the national press on some matter of importance.

In role-plays, the studio atmosphere with a number of television cameras and powerful lighting will all convey the reality of the actual experience people go through when being grilled on television.

All the interviews should be recorded and played back to the delegates so that prior perceptions can be discussed. The individual strengths and weaknesses can be analysed and suggestions made on how the latter can be eliminated. Some of the one-to-one interviews should be analysed on an individual basis so that personal tuition of a delegate's mannerisms and behaviour can be undertaken in an atmosphere of constructive and candid criticism.

Length and numbers on workshop: To cover the material and effectively develop the media interviewing skills of delegates, numbers on a workshop should be limited to six based on two tutors and one or two professional interviewers (if one or both tutors is not skilled in this area).

The workshop should ideally be held on a residential basis over a period of three days to cover the material described above and, in particular, to allow ample time for individual practice interviews, playback and evaluation of performance.

Review of progress: Unlike other types of training and development, the television and tape recorded interviews should not be wiped out but saved and given to the individual delegates. This will enable them to compare their real life performances when they face the cameras and interviewers with their workshop practice runs. They will be able to see what progress or mistakes they have made and note what they need to correct in future interviews.

Personal Media Perception
Questionnaire – 2

On pages 68-70 you will have found, and I hope completed, a Personal Media Perception Questionnaire as frankly and objectively as possible.

Please try once again to complete this, using a photocopy of the original questionnaire. This time you will do so with the benefit of having read the preceding units on how to handle the media whether it be the press, radio or television.

The reason for doing this a second time is so that you can compare your perceptions of the media as a result of a better knowledge and understanding of what journalists do. Have they changed? If so, for the better or the worse and why?

References

MACKAY, I. (1984). *A Guide to Listening*. British Association for Commercial and Industrial Education

DAY, R. (1961). *Television: A Personal Report*. Hutchinson

DAY, R. (1989). *Grand Inquisitor*. London: George Weidenfeld and Nicholson

LIDSTONE, J. (1991). *Manual of Sales Negotiation*. London: Gower

TIDMAN, P. (1988). *Broadcast Communications*. MCB University Press Selling and Managing Series, 5, 2. Northampton: MCB University Press

TIDMAN, P., LLOYD SLATER, H. (1992). *Tidman's Media Interview Technique*. Maidenhead: McGraw-Hill International (UK) Ltd.

Recommended   Reading

DAY, R. (1989). *Grand Inquisitor*, London: George Weidenfeld &
    Nicholson

LIDSTONE, J. (1985). *Making Effective Presentations (Audio
    Manual)*. Aldershot: Gower

MARGACH, J. (1978). *The Abuse of Power*. London: W. H. Allen &
    Co Ltd.

PEASE, A. (1981). *Body Language*. London: Sheldon Press

BLAND, M. AND MONDESIR, S. (1987). *Promoting Yourself on
    Television and Radio – 2nd edition*. London: Kogan Page

MACKAY, I. (1984). *A Guide to Listening*. London: British
    Association for Commercial and Industrial Education

TIDMAN, P., LLOYD SLATER, H. (1992). *Tidman's Media Interview
    Technique*. Maidenhead: McGraw-Hill International (UK)
    Limited